MAKING
HEART
"**ROUNDS**"

MAKING HEART "ROUNDS"

STORIES OF LONG TERM RELATIONSHIPS

DR. PATRICIA BAINES

ISBN 979-8-9854993-0-8 Paperback
ISBN 979-8-9854993-1-5 E-book

Book and cover design by Asya Blue Design

bainesauthor.com

This book is dedicated to my grandparents,
Hazel and Clarence Baines.

Their relationship was the first I recall celebrating longevity.

CONTENTS

FOREWORD

by Dr. Sheryl Heron

W hy do relationships last? Is it a mystery, destiny, or is it never to be understood? The answer resides in the reality of the question. We want to be there, in this relationship, through life's journey, so therefore we are. We journey together.

Relationships between two people willing to give and share themselves are a mystery, yet that is the essence of life's journey. We meet people along the way who perhaps speak to our soul in ways not understood. Yet, the magic happens, and the desire to share one's life journey with that person emerges. Maybe for a moment, but ah, how intriguing for a lifetime. That is for some to know and for others to explore.

When Patricia Baines, my best friend from Medical School, mentioned she was writing a book on the longevity of relationships, the intrigue of what keeps couples together for more than twenty-five years, she piqued my interest. Over her career, she was sure to find more than 100 couples who would tell their story of love, commitment, and the journey to stay married or partnered. I knew immediately that this book would be an uplifting read, particularly in these somber times. Times when the world has changed during the isolation of a pandemic.

This is not her first book to expound upon journeys of the heart. Her first book, *Seven Days, The Journey Home,* speaks in a powerful way of her dying nephew and her love for him as she navigated the pain and the suffering with her family. Walking with her through those days was a powerful testimony to the value of relationships. The relationship between an aunt and her nephew and our relationship has deepened through that journey together.

This book speaks to the power of relationships of a different kind. These couples' relationships, most of who Patricia met while working as a physician over two decades. From the beginning of medical school to today. Patricia has been determined to identify couples she met as patients while working in medicine. Couples she met in the various hospitals she has worked in over her career. Each of these couples detailed the secret for longevity in staying together through the years. Many couples were married, some were not, and all have stood the test of time. The secrets shared by the couples from commitment to the resonant "aha" of "you want to be there" keep it simple. To stay married, partnered, coupled to someone over time through sickness and health, you must simply want to be there.

If you are as curious as I was to read the stories, please do. You will laugh, perhaps cry, and without question be intrigued. Layering the question of longevity in relationships while working in medicine fills the soul. Seeing the beauty of this over time fills the heart.

Sheryl Heron, MD, MPH
Professor of Emergency Medicine, Atlanta, Ga
Dr. Heron is an Emergency Medicine Physician and
Associate Dean at Emory School of Medicine.

"For one human being to love another; that is perhaps the most difficult of all our tasks, the ultimate, the last test and proof, the work for which all other work is but preparation."

— Rainer Maria Rilke

THE JOURNEY OF LASTING LOVE

Ihave always been intrigued by longevity, whether relationships, life
itself, buildings, cars, furniture, etc. The question that continuously
swirls in my mind is, "What makes something last so long, exist forever, or what seems like forever?"

I owned a 1966 Ford Mustang when I first started thinking about this
collection of stories. My car is over forty years old, and it runs like it was built
yesterday. I love that car, and apparently, so do lots of other people. Whenever
my mother used to take it for a spin or to the car shop for me, passersby would
always stop her and ask, "Hey, lady, does your son want to sell that car?"

She would smile and say, "It's my daughter's car, and no, she will not
sell it!"

I started learning French late in life, thinking *this should be a piece
of cake*. At the end of the spring semester, my French class, along with
several other classes and friends of classmates, went to Europe. It was a
wonderful experience! My most memorable moments are gazing at and
admiring the grandiose buildings, the marble statues, and the details that
have lasted century after century. It begs the question, "Why aren't all
buildings constructed with the same materials and care that made the
buildings in Europe last forever?"

How This Book Came About

It was never my intent to actually write this book. By happenstance, I
experienced a moment of observed longevity between two people, the

Williams, who you'll meet shortly. This couple meant the world to each other; they were best friends, lovers, partners, husband, and wife. From that point and going forward, I was on a mission.

This is not a book of statistical data about relationships, making a relationship work, or even the top ten things for success in any relationship. This is a collection of excerpts from conversations and expressions of personal points of view shared with me over the years as an Emergency Medicine Physician as I spoke with my patients, their partner/significant other, mates, and their families about the longevity of their relationship.

There are no heroines or heroes, no one to rescue, and there are no bad guys or victims. There are funny exchanges, real feelings, candid answers, and a glimpse into someone's soul during a moment of their life when they were most vulnerable. Good health is significantly precious in life, and without it, a person can do little else. I have always been intrigued when I meet people who have been together for twenty-five plus years. It is not a magic number, but rather, it is the number that stuck in my mind when I asked people how long they have been together. In reality, nowadays, making it to five years seems like a feat, despite saying, "Till death do us part."

As an Emergency Medicine Physician, I often see people at their worst and their wit's end. "Good health is the one thing that, without it, you can do nothing else," said one of my Attending Physicians to us as a group of young medical students.

In this environment as patients—where people are the most helpless, not in control of their destiny, and under the stress of illness—I find people to be the most honest. With that awareness, I began my probing and asked patients who had been with their spouse/partner for twenty-five years or more, "How did you manage to stay together and to achieve such longevity?"

Over the years, I have met couples who have been married, divorced, and then remarried each other or another person. I spoke with couples who eloped, couples who had an arranged marriage, couples who had big or small weddings, and the infamous shotgun wedding. I talked with people who had civil unions, common-law marriages, and a couple who said their vows to each other in the silence and intimacy of the forest with no one else around.

I didn't have any preconceived ideas about the most frequent response, nor did I know that I would get such a broad range of answers. Conversely, I thought there would be a common theme, a common thread, some "Ah-ha! That is it, and yes, you are right" moments. Each time I presented the question, it was as if they had been waiting for someone to make such a significant inquiry. Answers spontaneously rolled off their tongues, and on some occasions, they were still talking as I was exiting the examination room.

One aspect that struck me was that each individual, no matter how long they had been together in general, had their own idea of "what was the key on how they achieved longevity." In some cases, one partner would nod their head in agreement with what the other was expressing, but they each had their own perspective regarding longevity.

There is no chronology per se to the stories other than they are a collection from four different countries: the United States, Jamaica, New Zealand, and Australia. As you read, you will see a hint of collectiveness or some common themes that build to create a picture of the requirements and traits of long-term love.

The stories are individual. They can be enjoyed all at once or over time, in order, or just a random peruse. You may decide to have a daily sneak peek into the thoughts of those behind these testaments of love and longevity.

THE BEST OF FRIENDS

Years ago, and too many to mention, I was a fourth-year medical student at Howard University in Washington, D.C. While I was training with the Internal Medicine service, it was my job to ensure that all of my patients' labs and x-rays were accounted for and results documented.

Mrs. Williams was my patient, and she had been in the hospital for several weeks. She'd had abdominal surgery, and it had been a rocky course. She was home for some time when she got sick and was admitted to the Medicine Team. In her late seventies, she was a fragile woman with smooth coco skin with streaks of gray woven through her coal-black hair, which was pulled back and plaited into one long braid. She had a pleasant face and always managed to smile when I entered the room. She was soft-spoken, and when Mr. Williams walked into the room, she perked up.

Mr. Williams was a stately gentleman, and *a gentleman was he*. He elegantly stood at six feet four inches, had perfect teeth and a smile that could melt away the woes of the day. He had a love for his wife like no other. He always walked in with his hat in hand and said, "Hello, young doctor," whenever he saw me. Then he would walk over to his wife, take her hand, and kiss her.

Sometimes he planted a gentle kiss on her hand and other times on her forehead. He spent hours by her bedside reading to her, sharing the details about his day, feeding her, and checking to see if she had enough covers on her feet. He said that she didn't like her feet to be cold. I smiled when he said that because I don't like my feet to be cold either.

The Williams' had been married for **fifty-three years**. The first time he asked her to marry him, she said no. He laughed when he told me that story. They only had one child, a daughter, killed in a car accident at twenty. There was still sadness in his voice when he spoke of their beloved daughter.

I had been with the Medicine Service for four weeks, but I felt as if I had known the Williams for a long time, and they seemed like family. I would smile as I observed that he was at her beck and call, even before she could ask for anything. It was as if he anticipated what she was about to say because he knew her so well.

Mr. Williams would joke. Using his index finger, he would tap the side of his head and say, "Young doctor, I can read her mind." As he spoke, his wife looked at him and blushed. I thought, *do women still blush after fifty-three years of being married to the same person? I guess they do.*

One Friday evening, as I was walking toward Mrs. Williams' room, her door was open. Mr. Williams walked out with his hat in his hand, and tears were streaming down his face. I ran to him and asked, "Mr. Williams, what's wrong?"

He shook his head and said, "Young doctor, I lost my best friend. She is gone."

I ran into Mrs. Williams' room, and there she laid, peacefully with her pleasant face. My heart sank, and tears rolled down my face. I wiped my face and ran out of the room to find Mr. Williams. I walked over to him and expressed my sorrow for his significant loss. I asked him if there was someone who I could call or something that I could get for him.

He sadly shook his head and declared, "I lost my best friend. She was the world to me, my wife."

I have never forgotten Mr. and Mrs. Williams. They were the inspiration and catalyst for my search for how and why people stayed in relationships for years. I marveled at the Williams'. Despite the stress of his wife's illness, the uncertainty of her fate, the loss of their daughter, and the years of all that life had brought their way, it was evident that Mr. Williams loved his wife. More striking was that he spoke of her as his best friend. He didn't say, "I lost my wife," but he said, "I lost my best friend."

I thought that must have been their secret why, after fifty-three years of marriage, he could still make Mrs. Williams blush.

GIVE SERVICE AND RESPECT

One evening, I walked into one of the examination rooms to see my next patient, Mr. Mendez, who was seventy-six years old. He had a terrible cough for several days and was, according to his wife, "being stubborn" about coming to the hospital. The couple said they had been married for **forty-six years**. When asked, "What's the secret," this was their response:

"Respect, even in anger. Respect the other person," said Mr. Mendez

Mrs. Mendez continued, "First thing in the morning, serve the other person."

As I walked out of the room, I thought, *did she mean literally or figuratively?*

BELIEVE IN WHAT'S POSSIBLE

When I was a resident-in-training, I recall speaking with a friend who stated that he didn't believe that he would ever get married or be committed to one person for a lifetime. He said it was "not normal." I remember him saying, "Look around you, and you will see the number of divorced people, and that is because you are asking a person to do something unnatural, which is to be confined and tied to another human being."

I looked at him askance and said, "You haven't met the right person yet. You may not want to get married, but you will want to be committed to that person."

He laughed and replied, "I will let you know."

NO ME, JUST WE

I met a couple who had been married for **forty years**. It was an arranged marriage, and the couple was from India. I inquired if they knew each other before the wedding, and they answered, "Yes."

However, when I asked if they wanted to marry each other, the husband said, "Yes," and the wife replied, "No. I was longing for another boy." She explained that you don't necessarily love the person you are arranged to marry, but eventually, you grow to love them.

I asked if there was a possibility that you may never grow to love that person. She momentarily pondered the question, and eventually, her response was, "Yes, I suppose so."

When asked about the longevity of their marriage, they had their individual responses.

She replied, "Compatibility, similar backgrounds, and respect."

Her husband's response was, "Once you become married, there is no 'me'—just 'we.' Keep the lines of communication open."

I thought this was different. Typically, it is the woman commenting about communication or the lack thereof.

LEARN TO LOVE EACH OTHER

In speaking with couples whose marriages were arranged, they often didn't know much about the other person, and they did not begin their relationship "in love." The common theme for the women was that you grow to love your chosen partner.

One woman told me that "falling in love" and then getting married was an "American ideal." She continued to inform me that the marriages in her native homeland, India, were based on who your parents thought would be good for you and whether the person came from a good family. She felt that parents were better at choosing partners for their children, as evidenced by her comment, "Your parents know you better than you know yourself." She also told me that arranged marriages have a lower divorce rate than non-arranged marriages.

At that time, I was unaware of any studies that compared the length of relationships in arranged marriages versus non-arranged marriages. However, I would venture to say that the pros and cons of this topic would, indeed, be a heated debate.

*"Love is the journey...
not the destination."*

DISTANCE MAKES A DIFFERENCE

I was walking down the corridor of the ER when one of my residents called me into the exam room to discuss a patient. She was concerned about not being able to locate a pulse in his right foot and its mottled appearance.

As the evening progressed, I learned that he had been married for **forty years** during my conversation with the patient. When asked, "What is your secret?" he looked up at me, raised his eyebrows, and replied, "I was always gone."

I wrote that on a bit of scrap paper, then I added, "Wife?" I wondered *if I had asked his wife the same question, what would have been her response?*

CELEBRATE A GREAT INSTITUTION

One day, I asked a colleague if he had any elderly patients he was seeing, and he answered, "No, and why?"

I told him that I was collecting data from people in relationships for twenty-five years or more to ask about their longevity. His response was, "Oh, wow! That's great!"

Subsequently, he said, "I think marriage is a great institution—if you like institutions."

I believe that he did since he was married.

BE IN THE SAME BOOK

Mrs. Edmonson was a spirited, seventy-three-year-old who came to the ER with her husband. Mr. Edmonson was the patient. He anxiously sat on the edge of the bed, and he let Mrs. Edmonson do all the talking. He wordlessly nodded in his wife's direction when I asked him what brought him in today. After addressing his issues, I asked if they minded telling me how long they had been married.

"It has been **forty-six years**," his wife replied.

"What is the secret to your longevity," I asked.

He replied, "Love, trust, and understanding."

She said, "You have to be in the 'same book,' you can't be in 'different books,' and you can't disagree with everything, but only some things." Then she added, "We had all boys."

That was the first time someone mentioned their children and differentiated their gender. I was thrown for a loop. Was having male children part of the secret? Did she think that they were easier to raise, or was it merely a fact that she was adding?

BE A SECRET WEAPON—
PRACTICE PURE LOVE

O ne day I was sitting behind the nurse's station when the paramedics came in with a ninety-two-year-old woman. She was beautiful with smooth caramel skin tone, fine lines at the corner of her eyes, and a head full of gray hair that fell to her shoulders. She didn't look a day over sixty. She was a petite woman who reminded me of my paternal grandmother, who we affectionately called "Big Momma," although she was just five feet tall.

She was having leg pain, which made walking difficult. The paramedics stated that her husband was probably looking for somewhere to park. After introducing myself, she smiled and asked if her husband was there. I informed her that I believed he was trying to park the car.

"Okay," she replied.

After questioning her about what brought her to the Emergency Room and conducting a physical exam, I told her that we had to run some tests, do an ultrasound of her leg, and get blood work done. I explained that I was concerned about her leg and needed to ensure that she had not developed a blood clot.

She said, "Sugar, do just what you need to, you are the doctor, and I trust you."

When I returned to her bedside again, she asked whether her husband had made it to the hospital yet. I told her that I would check. As I turned to walk toward the door, a gentleman appeared. He was about five feet and ten inches tall, wearing a well-worn brown fedora, brown slacks, and a crisp, white shirt with suspenders. He was ninety-four years old with good upright posture, sharp, and looked as young as his wife. Her face instantly lit up the room when he graced the doorway.

She blurted out, "There's my man," and she winked at him.

He deftly removed his hat and replied, "That's my girl!"

"Come here, Sugar," she said, and he walked to the side of her bed and kissed her on the lips.

I was smiling so much that my cheeks hurt! Had I not witnessed this exchange firsthand, I might have thought that they were auditioning for a part in a movie! Of course, you know exactly what I was thinking. They are perfect for my next subjects for the probing question, what was the secret to their longevity?

After all her tests were completed, I entered the room to speak with them. I told her and her husband that she had a blood clot in her leg. As I looked at her, I informed her that she would need to stay in the hospital for a few days.

Her husband stood up and exclaimed, "Aw shoot! I can't take her home with me!"

His facial expression conveyed a deep disappointment to the degree that I felt terrible for him. I told him that maybe he could stay with his wife. She shook her head to indicate "No."

She proceeded to say, "You should go home. I will be alright."

He lamented, "This will be the first time in all our years of marriage that we won't sleep in the same bed, and I am not sure that I could even fall asleep."

She grinned and said, "Ain't he somethin'!"

I inquired how long they had been married.

Nodding his head before speaking, he said, "We have been married **sixty-six years**," gazing in her direction. She was shaking her head in unison.

I was still smiling with admiration and deep appreciation as I observed all the unspoken words between them. I was compelled to ask, "What's your secret?"

He stated, "She is the secret weapon, and whatever she says goes."
She just laughed and said, "Yeah."

A couple of days later, I checked on her to ensure that she was improving. She was doing well and was sent home. My thoughts circling back to Mr. and Mrs. Williams, I was delighted and simultaneously relieved.

TAKE TIME APART

At three o'clock in the morning, when a patient comes into your Emergency Room, you have to believe that whatever is going on cannot wait, but that is not always the case. In this instance, with this patient, it couldn't wait. He came in with his wife, pushing him in a wheelchair. He was in obvious distress as he leaned forward to the right and was about to fall out of the wheelchair. I met them in the hallway and asked what was going on with him.

His wife replied, "He woke up with severe pain on his right side and broke out into a sweat."

He was put on a gurney, had an IV placed, bloods taken, given pain medication, and a CAT scan was ordered since I was concerned about him having a kidney stone.

I spoke with the patient and his wife to tell them that he probably had a kidney stone. I explained what we were doing and assured them that I would check back in a few minutes to see if his pain had settled. Upon my return to the patient's room, I saw that he was, feeling much better.

Smiling, he told me, "Whatever you gave me was a miracle, and I would give you a kiss if I didn't think my wife would get jealous."

His wife smiled as she thanked me before saying, " kidney stones, that's God's answer to childbirth, so men can have a sneak peek at what women go through during labor."

He replied, "God is smart, and it is a good thing that women bear children. Otherwise, there would not be any children in the world because men couldn't handle it." He shook his head and declared, "I thought I was going to die."

While his wife burst into laughter, she managed to exclaim, "See how dramatic men are!"

As I spoke with this couple, I learned that they had been married for **thirty years**. When asked what is the secret to their longevity?

He said, "We always took separate vacations."

She agreed. She said, "It gives you time for yourself, and you develop more appreciation for each other." As she spoke, he nodded in agreement.

This was the only couple I spoke with that not only agreed with each other but also reached the same conclusion: *it appears that absence makes the heart grow fonder*.

LIVE A GOOD LONG LIFE

I have intermittently shared with my colleagues in the ER that I was doing this data gathering. Their responses were always one of surprise, and they thought it was a great idea! Several of my colleagues would inform me that they had a candidate for me. They would see if I was working that shift and say, "Hey, I got one for you." I thought that was funny because I felt as if I was part of a clinical trial.

In the beginning, I expressed my fascination with longevity, which was the catalyst for my quest. While most of the patients I spoke with were couples, I also inquired with my geriatric population. Several were over the age of ninety and still going strong.

My first encounter with an elderly gentleman over the age of ninety and someone who was not my paternal grandfather, who lived to the age of ninety-eight–was an entertaining man, 103 years old. I was a medical student on the Family Practice service at that time. Before going into the room, I picked up the chart to review the patient's information, such as name, age, the reason for visit, etc. I thought it was a mistake that the chart indicated that the patient was 103 years old, walking, talking, and not taking any medications. I must be dreaming!

I entered the room to find a gentleman about five feet four inches, close haircut, no mustache, or beard, standing up and reading one of the posters on the wall.

He turned as I entered the room and said, "Mornin', young lady."

I introduced myself, informed him that I was a medical student, and I would be taking care of him today. I was captivated by him from the moment he spoke, and he was full of stories. You can imagine that you must have volumes of stories to tell after over 100 years of living and you are still upright and coherent!

He was at the clinic because he had trouble getting rid of his persistent cough.

He said, "This old, stubborn cough is giving me a fit."

He came to the clinic at the insistence of his great-granddaughter, who accompanied him. With concern and evident affection, she said, "Great-granddaddy, that's too much coughing for a little man like you."

He smiled and said, "She is a bossy little thing. I just love her to death."

He said, "Student-doctor when I was a young man, I used to work part-time at a grocery store and bagged groceries for a little pocket change. One day, I was leaving work, and some guys hit me on my head and robbed me. I had to leave that job."

I asked, "How old were you when that happened?"

He replied, "I was sixty-seven."

I laughed and said, "At 103, I guess sixty-seven is young."

I asked, "What is your secret to living such a long life?"

He answered, "God has been good to me. I was a crazy young man, but I got straightened out." He smiled and said, "Yeah, I was something else, and I surprised myself that I lived to be this old and grey."

The funny thing was that he didn't have completely grey hair. Though it was cut close, I could see it was salt and pepper in color.

"Love, uplift, and inspire each other."

KEEP YOUR FAMILY CLOSE

One afternoon, I walked into one of our Critical Care Bays to see a patient, and as I was passing by another patient, a family member asked if the patient could have some water. I asked the patient her name and said I would check with her doctor to see if it was okay for her to drink. She was there because fluid was building up in her lungs, a condition known as congestive heart failure. As a result, her doctor didn't want her to have water at the moment, but she could have a few ice chips.

As I spoke with the patient and her family, I discovered that she had just celebrated her 100th birthday two months earlier. She was stunning as the light bounced off her beautiful grey hair. She was virtually wrinkle-free, had hazel brown eyes, and still had all her teeth.

I asked her why I was not invited to her century celebration, for I would have attended.

She smiled and said, "If I had known, you could have come."

She was mentally sharp and could tell you anything you wanted to know. She knew the names of her medications, which were not many. Nevertheless, she knew them. I have thirty and forty-something-year-old patients who cannot tell me the name of even one of their medications.

On a couple of occasions, I went back to the Critical Care Bay to check on my patient, and I noticed there was always a family member close to the 100-year-old patient I spoke with earlier. This one particular time, as I passed by, the patient motioned for me to come to her bedside.

"This is my great-niece," she announced, "and she is more like my daughter." Her niece nodded in agreement as she smiled at her great aunt.

"Yes, you two are definitely related. I can see the striking resemblance," I said.

"Strong genes," was the patient's succinct reply.

I asked the patient, "What is your secret to such longevity?"

She motioned for me to come even closer, and I leaned in toward her. She revealed, "I never married," and then she winked at me!

Her great-niece laughed heartily and said, "She always says that."

The patient had the last say and stated, "Because it is true!"

I thought *I believe her*.

KID AROUND

Sometimes people tell you things that truly catch you off guard, and you don't know whether to laugh, hide the shock on your face, comment, or remain speechless. One day, I was taking care of a seventy-five-year-old woman who lost her footing and slipped. She broke her arm and needed a splint. She was in great spirits about the entire situation. She told me about a rug that she had been contemplating for months to get rid of for the reason of possibly falling.

She said, "I kept telling Birch, her husband, that one day I am going to break my neck by slipping on that old rug." She raised her eyebrows and said in an authoritative tone, "You know that rug is in the trash now, don't you?"

I knowingly smiled and replied, "Yes, ma'am."

I discovered that she had been married for **fifty-two years**. I asked her what was the secret of their long marriage?

She said, "Honey, you just do what you can do, and after that, if they don't like it, they can do it themselves." After sharing her insight, she gave a grand laugh, and I laughed with her.

After being discharged, she came down the hall and thanked me for her care. She nudged me and whispered, "Sometimes you have to beat the shit out of them every now and then. You know what I mean."

She gave a quick, little nod and threw her hand up in the air, waving goodbye as she walked toward the waiting room.

I was completely surprised! I just shook my head and laughed as I watched her strut down the hall and disappear around the corner. I thought *she is kidding. I **hope** she is just kidding.*

NEVER GIVE UP

I spoke with a man who had been with his wife for **twenty-seven years**. His wife's brother recently died, and she was having a difficult time. I asked him what had kept their marriage going for so many years. He admitted, "I am stubborn, and I don't like to fail. It is commitment, love, and compromise. He continued, I grew up in a single-parent home, and I made a commitment that I would have a complete family. Communication is key." He added, "We still have our problems."

I pondered his statement, "I don't like to fail." Was that an integral factor relative to marital longevity? If so, to what degree or specifically, what percentage? More questions came to mind. *Do you continue the course due to your motivation of not wanting to fail or because of the previously mentioned commitment, love, and compromise? Which way does the scale tip?*

SAY NO MORE

In speaking with a woman who had been with her husband of **forty years**, she concisely summed it up in one word, "Perseverance." Then she chuckled and said, "Need I say more?"

HAPPINESS AND LONGEVITY ARE NOT MUTUALLY EXCLUSIVE

As I listen to the voices and gather the spoken words of the patients and people I encounter, I think that longevity in any setting—relationships or work—must have some fundamental anchor. Is there something, someone, some ideology or group of ideas that allows you to maintain a constant walk on the same path for years?

Please don't be confused. I am not equating longevity with happiness. I anticipate that if I asked the question, "What makes you happy in your relationship," I would have received an entirely different set of answers. Further, I would venture to say that, comparatively speaking, I would have encountered more pause and contemplation from those who might have been involved in this happiness-related conversation as opposed to the feedback that I received regarding longevity.

I presume longevity and the sum of its parts house a finite percentage in the role of happiness. However, in no way are the two mutually exclusive. One can exist without the other.

DON'T AIM FOR PERFECT

My unofficial longevity demographic target is twenty-five years or more. However, I spoke with a woman who had been married **twenty-four years and a few months**. She stated that the secret to her longevity was, "We are perfectly matched, and I like him as a person."

Did "perfectly matched" mean "identical" in every way, or did that mean his scarcities were her strengths and vice versa? Was it a yin and yang relationship? The word "perfect" has always been daunting, except when I saw it at the top of a homework assignment or test.

As I walked away, I pulled a tiny notepad out of my lab coat pocket and wrote down the woman's feedback and my questions. Subsequently, I wrote, "Husband?"

This was the first time I heard the word "perfect" used.

"Love is friendship that has caught fire. It is quiet understanding, mutual confidence, sharing and forgiving."

— Ann Landers

Zenaida and Ivan Rosario,
married thirty-seven years—Stay Close

PUTTING COUPLEDOM FIRST

"We didn't have children" was the first statement that rolled off the tongue of a woman married for **thirty years.** She was not one of my patients, but she shared her insights. "You have to be tolerant of deficiencies," she continued. "You become one."

I asked her if there was a time when one or the other wanted children.

She replied, "One day, we sat down and talked about kids. We both came to the conclusion that our lives would be okay without them." Then she reflectively stated, "I think we would have ended in divorce if we would have had children because we have very different fundamental thoughts of how children should be raised."

Typically, you hear, "We stayed together for so long because of our child/children." Or, on the other end of the spectrum, the relationship broke up because one wanted children and the other didn't, or the woman got pregnant, and the man left.

Examining the longevity of commitment, pledge, or promise of a human being to another piques my curiosity and calls to mind additional questions. Do the same verbal reflections transcend all levels or forms of relationships? How about in the context of best friends or siblings?

TAKE ONE DAY AT A TIME

Sometimes you walk into a room, and you see a patient lying on the gurney that looks "much too good to need emergency medical care." But any good doctor worth their salt knows *looks* can occasionally be deceiving. My eighty-two-year-old patient looked fresh as the day and was cheerful as ever. She was having some issues with her bowels and feeling extremely tired. Unfortunately, it was bad news.

She has been married to her husband for **sixty-six years**, and they have six children.

Her thoughts about the longevity of their marriage were, "You go to work and come home. You do what you have to do," she said.

Her husband listened as he shook his head from side to side. He stated, "You take it a day at a time."

I asked, who is the oldest?

She smiled and quickly pointed to her husband.

WEATHER THE STORMS

As I entered one of the exam rooms in our Fast-Track area, a woman was sitting on the bed and reading a book. Upon entering, she looked up as I called her name. I introduced myself and asked what brought her here to the Emergency Room.

I discovered that it was going to be her **forty-fifth wedding anniversary** in two months. I inquired how she managed almost forty-five years with the same person.

She shook her head and said, "He was a stone alcoholic. I just prayed, and God heard my prayers. We have four kids, fifteen grandchildren, and four great-grandchildren. He doesn't drink no more."

I definitely believe that you need to have some level of faith, spirituality, or belief to weather through all the peaks and valleys. That applies to any relationship.

WORK HARD, BEHAVE

A gentleman I spoke with was in his second marriage, and they had been married for **twenty-six years**. He stated, "You work hard and do what you are told."

I wondered, *had he learned this lesson from his first marriage?*

BE PLAYFUL IN YOUR COMMUNICATION

In conversing with a gentleman fifty-four years of age and his male partner, who was a few years younger, they revealed that they had been together for **thirty-four years**. When questioned about their longevity, the couple had the following to say.

The first gentleman stated, "Remember, it's important to put the other person first." With a playful expression, he exclaimed, "and a rousing sex life doesn't hurt at all!" He laughed heartily as his partner shook his head as if to say, "I cannot believe that you said that!"

Then his partner chimed in, "Communication. If you stop or neglect to communicate, you might as well give it up." His final point was accentuated as he threw his hands up.

TAKE SOME ELEVATOR TIME

A gentleman who came to the ER because he was losing his vision. I examined him and told him that he would need to see the ophthalmologist upstairs. He was in the exam room alone, and I wasn't sure if he was accompanied to the hospital. Somehow, we got on the subject of marriage, and he told me he had been married for **forty-two years**.

Unprovoked, he said, "I do everything my wife tells me." He laughed, then looked at me and asked if his wife could come in.

The nurse called out to the waiting room for his wife as I went to tend to another patient.

The nurse escorted them upstairs to the eye clinic.

Upon her return, she smiled and said, "Dr. Baines, guess what? You know that couple that I took to the eye clinic?"

"Yes," I replied.

The nurse shared, "When we got into the elevator, he looked at her and said, 'You know what we do every time we get in an elevator. We kiss, so what's different now?' His wife laughed, and then they kissed!" The nurse expressed, "I thought that was so special!"

GO FIGURE

I encountered a ninety-five-year-old man who presented to the ER with red itchy eyes. He said, "I just don't know what happened to my eyes. Just as red as fire."

He told me he and his seventy-year-old wife had been married for **forty years**. When I asked about the longevity of their marriage, he said, "I don't know," as he hunched his shoulders.

I looked in his wife's direction and inquired what she thought.

Her reply was, "I don't have nothing to say. Everybody can figure it out for themselves."

"She thinks she is still a little girl," he remarked as he laughed and looked at her.

NOTEWORTHY SIMILARITIES

I spoke with a patient who had been married for **twenty-five years**. This was his second marriage, he said. He told me that his secret to longevity was, "Work hard and do what you are told."

I thought it was odd that I would get similar thoughts in the same week and only days apart from two men who were on their second marriage. It was noteworthy and struck me. As a result, I thought is this a recurring theme? I kept vigilant to see if there were any others in this cohort.

SHARING AND BEING

I attended a seventy-eight-year-old man whose wife of **forty-eight years** recently suffered from a brain aneurysm.

He said, "The key is friendship. We have a lot of things in common. We always had fun doing things together. I like being with my wife."

In a shy manner, her response was, "Love your partner and share things together."

JUST BEING TOGETHER

I spoke with my mother, who had been married for **thirty-three years** in her second marriage, although her late husband had passed. I asked about her view on longevity.

She said, "Good communication. We did many things together. Partied and socialized, took walks together. When you are together for a long time, you begin to think alike."

"Let us be grateful to people who make us happy, they are the charming gardeners who make our souls blossom."

— Marcel Proust

WEAR THE PANTS AND BE A PRANKSTER

I met a female couple who was celebrating **forty-one years** of commitment. We discuss the longevity of their relationship.

The first woman said, "I wear the pants and pull out the chair," and proceeded to laugh uncontrollably.

The second woman looked at her partner and said, "Always the jokester".

The first woman spoke again. Pointing to her partner, she said, "She is always right. Really."

Her partner replied, "The key, talking everything out. You have to. Communication is key."

KNOW WHAT REAL LOVE MEANS

The man lying on the gurney had diabetes, and he was concerned about his extraordinarily elevated blood sugar. He said that he needed to be able to work. He was in his work attire, and he had grease under his nails.

I soon discovered that he had been married for **forty-three years**.

His words of wisdom were, "You have to be kind, gentle and don't hurt one another's feelings. That's real love," he professed.

HAVE STIFF DISAGREEMENTS, NOT ROWS

I walked into the room, and sitting upright on the bed was an eighty-eight-year-old elegant queen who looked very regal in her tailored suit. Her daughter accompanied her to the Emergency Room because her blood pressure was elevated.

She told me she had been married for **sixty-five years**. I was impressed, and I had to shake her hand. Exclaiming as I sat down, "Shut the front door! That's more years than I have been alive!"

She laughed and said, "We never argued, but we had some stiff disagreements," and she laughed even more.

Her daughter commented, "God has blessed them."

"Indeed, he has," I agreed. I smiled and thought, *I like that "stiff disagreements."*

FIND WAYS OF LOVING

The seventy-three-year-old man I was attending had pneumonia and visually looked ill. His wife of **fifty-three years** was at his side. When asked how they stayed together for fifty-three years, she said, "I love him, and he loves me, but in a different way. We all have our way of loving each other."

A *"different way?"* I thought. Although I didn't ask her what she meant by that, I certainly wondered.

NO SNEAKING

I had a twist of events because my next spokesperson on the subject of longevity was not my patient, but rather, she was the sister of my patient. She was seventy-seven years old and accompanied her younger sister, my patient. She told me that her husband had recently died of pancreatic cancer and that they were three months short of their **fifty-fifth wedding anniversary**.

She said, "The key is to love each other and don't do the things that you are not supposed to do, like sneak around. You aren't supposed to do that."

Dr. Sushil Sachdev and Kamlesh Sachdev,
married forty years — No Me, Just We

FORGIVE, FORGIVE, AND FORGIVE AGAIN

There was a man whose wife recently had neck surgery, and they had been married for **fifty-seven years**. He stated that their secret was "give and take." He indicated, "For every little thing that goes wrong, you can't fly off the handle. You have to forgive, and they will forgive."

He then erupted with laughter as his belly moved up and down. He expressed, "The man has to be a little henpecked, and the woman has to be a little rooster pecked!"

He continued saying, "Also do things that the other one likes, even if you don't care for it."

He finished with, "It's alright to disagree, but don't be disagreeable. Say, 'Well, let's take a look at it,' and then *actually* take a look at it."

WHATEVER SHE SAYS

As I entered the room, I saw a spry eighty-nine-year-old woman with green eyes that seemed to dance, sitting on the bed looking at the fishhook in her thumb. She looked disgusted as she said in astonishment, "I just can't believe I did this."

She had been fishing and somehow managed to impale herself with a fishhook. As I talked with her and proceeded to remove the fishhook from her thumb, she told me she had been married for **forty years**. Her response to her secret of longevity was, "There's no secret." She said, "Let him do what he wants to do."

I imagine that there are a lot of eyebrows that might be raised at that statement and perhaps equally as many, "Yeah, that's right," emphatic retorts from men. That is not a fight that I would referee.

"A kiss is a lovely trick designed by nature to stop speech when words become superfluous."

— Ingrid Bergman

TAKE THE RIGHTEOUS PATH

The man in the wheelchair being brought to the gurney looked up at me and said, "Doc, if it weren't for these tennis shoes, I wouldn't be here. I have worn boots since I left the army." He continued, "My grandchildren bought these tennis shoes for me. I wore them, out of not wanting to hurt their feelings. Now, look where I am, at the hospital, because I tripped in these things and hurt my knee. Hope I didn't break anything at my age."

Upon examining his right knee, I felt a large amount of fluid. Since he could not move that leg in either direction, I sent him for an x-ray and subsequently removed some fluid so that he could freely move his knee.

I learned that he had been married for **forty years**.

Sharing his analysis for longevity, he said, "You just do what you are supposed to do and hope that the other person does what they are supposed to do."

YOU HAVE TO WANT TO BE THERE

As I entered room three, a gentleman adjusted the covers on a female patient as she lay in bed. I observed that she was shivering, and she didn't look well. The couple was in their seventies. She felt weak and unwell, and he was very attentive to her. He was a tall, thin man with a smooth, caramel complexion.

He took a seat and crossed his legs as I approached the bed. I introduced myself, asked the patient her name, and then inquired who the gentleman was. He was her husband of **fifty-four years**. After examining the patient, I explained the plan to her. He proceeded to give me background information on his wife regarding her medical history and the events of her past few days.

He stood up again, went to her bedside, stroked her hair, and gently asked, "Honey, are you okay?"

She mutely nodded. Once again, he sat down.

They had been married for fifty-four years, and it is noteworthy that they got married the year I was born.

He shared his insightful key to their longevity when he said, "You have to *want* to be there," with a noticeable emphasis on "want."

As he sat in the chair, leaning back with his legs crossed, he nodded his head and punctuated his perspective with the statement, "That's right."

She faintly whispered, "Prayer and love the Lord."

I informed them that she would need to be admitted to the hospital, and she was not thrilled about the news.

He sighed and said, "Honey, we have to do whatever it takes to get you well."

I walked out of the room and had an epiphanic moment. I sat and thought, *that's it—that is very true! You have to **want** to be there! Because, at the end of the day, if you don't want to put your key in the door and go inside, nothing else matters. Wow!*

I shared my remarkable epiphany with a colleague who was working alongside me.

He said, "Yes, that guy is pretty insightful."

TAKE WHAT YOU NEED

The fifty-seven-year-old male patient appeared to be asleep when I entered. I called out his name, and he turned toward me as he opened his eyes. He was there because his blood pressure was very low. I looked in the direction of the visitor sitting facing the patient's back. "May I ask your relationship to the patient," I queried.

"That's my husband," was her reply.

He propped himself up on his elbows, slightly looked over his shoulder, and asked, "What did she say?"

I stated, "She said she is your wife." I laughed, and with a smile, I said to her, "You have your hands full."

She smiled back and nodded.

He claimed, "She is stubborn. Had to make her love me."

I glanced in his direction and asked, "How long have you been married?"

She proclaimed, "Sounds like too long."

He stated, "Married **thirty-two years**."

I turned toward her for confirmation, and she nodded.

Once again, he propped himself up and asked, "What did she say?"

I smiled because of their bantering, and I said, "I asked, 'What's the key to your longevity?'"

Then she said, "You really need to listen."

He acquiesced by saying, "Just say 'yes.'"

To that, she replied, "Smart man."

I thought that was the end of the conversation, but then she interjected as she crossed her legs and stated with a matter-of-fact tone, "I take what I need and leave the rest."

SIT DOWN AND EAT

When I walked in, a female patient was looking at something on the other side of the exam room curtain. I peeked around the curtain, and a tall, wry gentleman was wearing a light brown suit and thick, black-rimmed eyeglasses. They were at church when his wife began to have neck spasms as she listened to him sing in the all-male choir. They had been married for **thirty years**, and he shared his thoughts on longevity.

"You have to do things together, and we talk a lot," he said. "I don't feel like I have to be right, and she don't feel like she has to be right. Compromise."

She added, "It's what you make out of it."

He then told the story of how they came to be a couple.

He said, "Her mother put us back together. When we first met, we got along so well that we were afraid it wasn't real. One evening, her mother said, 'Come and get some of this barbecue.' I told her mother that me and Pat just quit. We had broken up. Her mother said, 'Come get this barbecue,' and we have been eating barbecue ever since. I think we were both afraid of commitment."

COME WHAT MAY

The gentleman sitting on the bed didn't appear a day over sixty, but he was actually seventy-one years old. Two years his senior, his wife was sitting in the chair next to his bed. He had swelling in both of his legs and was starting to experience some shortness of breath. After attending to the patient, I was told they had been married **forty-eight years** and counting.

Her perspective on longevity was "Loving each other," and she added, "putting up with whatever comes."

Once she finished, he told her, "Honey, I want a peppermint."

As she put one in his mouth, I joked by asking, "Are you going to charge him for that?"

She laughed as she said, "I should. The next one, I will."

He interrupted as he smiled, "We have been together for forty-eight years, and she charged me all right."

She laughed.

His insight on longevity, he said, "I don't know." Then he expressed, "Just stay together."

DO YOUR PART

I had a patient who was eighty-three years old. She told me that she takes care of her mother, 105 years old. "My mother is healthier than me," she said, and then she laughed.

The patient had been married for **twenty-two years** to her late husband, and she said, "You just have to trust in the Lord."

They had six children, of which five were girls and one boy.

She said, "I just ain't able to do everything, and you just do your part." As she sat up to put on her purple beanie hat, with conviction, she said, "I haven't given up yet."

She was pretty adorable, had a big smile albeit no teeth, and had very few wrinkles when she furrowed her brow. She said that the secret was children. "I never remarried. I didn't want anyone over my kids, she stated directly."

KNOW WHEN YOU'RE JUST PLAIN LUCKY

My next patient was a seventy-year-old man who looked worn and came to the hospital for weakness. He had a great sense of humor, and it was evident that he was a jokester. He and his wife had been married for **fifty-three years**.

As for the question of longevity, she said, "To stay together for this long, you have to close your eyes and pray."

He laughed and said, "Be a good husband. Also, tell her, remind her that she is lucky to have me for a husband." He let out a barreling laugh.

She smiled as she shook her head. It was clear that she was accustomed to his antics.

As he laugh, he said, "Yeah, so when she starts to fuss, she will think, Oh, yeah! I am lucky to be married to him."

BE THERE

After hearing that the couple had been married for **forty years**, I delved into the familiar question at hand. She looked in her husband's direction and succinctly stated, "We love each other." He said, "You have to want to be there."

'As stated by a previous patient's husband, he spoke those same identical seven words that still profoundly impacted me. I went to the workstation computer sat in a chair, and shared with a different colleague the dialogue that had just taken place.

She nodded in the affirmative as she said, "Simple but powerful words."

Once again, I thought, *in reality, if you don't want to be there, then nothing else matters.*

Just say, "Love ya!"

THE BEST WAY

This story is not from a patient of mine, but I love the humor. This couple had been married **forty-two years**.

When I asked about longevity, she said, "Genuine love. You have to respect each other, show love, and be there for each other. We have known each other since high school."

Her husband laughed and said, "She couldn't stand me when she first met me. She would always call me 'boy.' She would say, 'Boy, I can't stand you.'" He laughed even more. "But I wore her down," he stated proudly. "She would come with her mother to the meat market where I used to work, and I would give her mother a good cut of meat. Her mother would say, 'That's a nice, young man.' She would look at her mom and turn her head. I thought, yeah! I'm getting there!" Then he looked at his wife of forty-two years with an affectionate smile.

His response to the question of longevity was, "I just do what she tells me." He smiled and said, "That's the best way to be."

HARMONIOUS ENERGY PERSISTS

I had a fifty-six-year-old gentleman who came to the ER due to blurred vision. He was driving at the time and had to pull off the road. When he arrived, his blood pressure was very high, 229/140.

After taking care of him to get his blood pressure under control, I found out he had been married **thirty-five years**. His wife had arrived and was sitting at his bedside, by this time. She was beautiful with golden brown short hair that was brushed back.

He said, "I was probably mad at her today when I left." He laughed and continued, "That's probably why my blood pressure went up." They both laughed.

She revealed, "When I got the call that he was here, I had to decide whether to play golf with a friend or come to the hospital. I decided to come to the hospital."

They laughed in unison.

He said, "For thirty-five years, we have listened to each other and been respectful."

She said, "Prayer and respect. You can't give up."

Then she shared that her dad's last name was the same as mine. "He was awarded a Purple Heart in the Gulf War," she said. "He wouldn't go get it."

Her husband looked at her and said as he laughed, "You mean I almost married a celebrity?"

The energy between this husband and wife was vivacious. Their playfulness was great to watch.

DIFFERENT PERSPECTIVES ON LONGEVITY

I took care of a seventy-nine-year-old man with gray streaks through his hair and wearing round wire-rimmed glasses. I finished examining him and exited the room. When I returned, a woman was sitting in the chair next to him. I introduced myself and asked, "Are you his wife?"

"Yes," was her response.

The patient was lying on his side with his back to her. He raised himself up and inquired, "What did she say?"

I responded, "She said 'Yes.'"

He mumbled, "Oh! I didn't hear her."

Later, I asked them, "How long have you been married?"

He replied, "**Forty years**." Then he looked at her and said, "Isn't that right?" He then stated, "The key is keeping my mouth shut." He laughed, and she laughed with him.

Her response was, "It's ninety percent give on the wife's part, and ten percent take."

With an amused expression, he said, "I didn't know that." They both laughed.

"Yeah! That's right," she said.

TAKE GOOD CARE OF EACH OTHER

A sixty-four-year-old man was sitting in one of the bays, waiting to be seen. It turned out that he had been married **forty-four years.**

He said, "The secret to longevity is to marry a good woman." He explained, "I have been treating her right for a long time. She knows it too. I am a good man and take good care of my family. Now, it is time for them to take care of themselves." He shook his head with a woeful expression, and added, "Especially my oldest daughter."

HAVE LOVE, FAITH, AND TEAMWORK

KB, a seventy-five-year-old woman, who came to the ER after a fall while attending an Expo, was extremely chatty. Though she had pain in her shoulder and lower back from the fall, she felt that her pride—was hurt—more than her body. Still, it was apparent that she was in pain. She was there with her husband of **thirty years**. This was the second marriage for both of them.

She teased, "After ten years, he asked me to marry him." She continued, "The key to staying together for thirty years is love. You know, we are best friends, and he was a great boyfriend. We are both Christians, Catholic."

He agreed, "Love is the key." He went on to say, "You have to always help each other, be there for each other."

I interjected, "Like a team."

"Yeah," he said. "You have to love each other, even when you feel like punching the other person's lights out," he laughed heartily. "You have to have love, and I love her to death!"

Then I asked her, "May I use your name in my book?"

"Yes," she said, "I would be honored."

DO THE BEST YOU CAN

A male patient came in after having a choking episode. He grew up in Jamaica, and his wife was from Trinidad. The couple had been married for **forty-six years**, and she shared her view about those number of years.

"We never quarreled over money, although we had financial hardships," she explained. "We had children, so we had to share a slice of bread or a cup of tea, but we never quarreled about money. You do the best you can." She paused to reflect, and then she said, "I don't know if there is a secret."

I looked in his direction. He was looking at his wife and didn't comment.

I didn't probe any further.

SOMETIMES YOU NEED TO TURN A DEAF EAR

My sixty-five-year-old patient had been married to his wife for **forty-five years**. I thought in amazement, *gee, he has been married for more than half his lifetime!*

He quickly told me, "Tolerance is what you need to stick things out."

Afterward, he complained about needing to be admitted overnight into the hospital.

His wife's response to his complaining was, "Ignore him," she said. "I work with kids all day, so I had to ignore him the first half of our marriage."

LOVE, JOY, PEACE, AND THE LORD JESUS CHRIST

Salt and pepper hair, with very kind eyes, is how I would describe my eighty-nine-year-old patient, who had been married to his ninety-three-year-old wife for **sixty years**. He was in the ER because he was having problems swallowing.

His wife didn't accompany him. He said that it was too late in the evening, and he didn't want her to be out of the house this late. He told me that they have three daughters and three sons.

With emphatic conviction, he stated, "Love, joy, peace, and the Lord Jesus Christ is the key to longevity."

"Amen," I whispered.

BRING HOME THE BACON

The gentleman lying on the hospital bed was a handsome, stately, seventy-five years old with silvery hair. He presented to the ER because he was experiencing episodes of nausea and vomiting. He had dropped a heavy jar on his foot a couple of weeks earlier, and now he had an infection in that foot.

"Initially, my foot was just swollen and painful," he said, "and then the swelling got better, and the pain was less."

His wife was with him, and I dubbed her "Silver Fox" because she had a mane of gray hair, pulled up just so. She had the smoothest dark complexion and wore small, rectangular eyeglasses. I thought *I hope that when my gray comes in, it looks as stunning on me as it does on her*.

As for his thoughts regarding longevity, he said, "You have to keep doing what you do, and you have to keep a little courtship. I drove a Marta bus for twenty-seven years, and a man's thing to do is bring home the bacon. I was a country boy."

She elaborated by saying, "He never let me work." Then she threw her head back as she laughed and confessed, "I worked anyway. I had a daycare. He doesn't know this, but I did lawn care, and I had a cleaning business too. Sometimes, I didn't tell him everything. He didn't need to know everything." She continued, "You really have to love them, not money. Forgive and forget. Get to know the person. We are from similar backgrounds." She extolled, "He would always stand up for me, and we were determined to stay married."

"Love is an act of endless forgiveness, a tender look which becomes a habit."

— Peter Ustinov

KNOW HOW IT WORKS

"I have something stuck in my throat," the seventy-three-year-old gentleman explained to me as I approached his bedside. He was alone, but his wife of **thirty-three years** was en route. Taking the opportunity to gauge the male perspective without his wife present, I asked, "How have you managed thirty-three years?"

He replied, "You pay the bills and be quiet. No use keepin' on talking." He continued, "Lots of my friends say they run the house. They don't run the house. They *think* they run it." He knowingly smiled as he shook his head.

When his wife arrived, I expressed, "Congratulations on thirty-three years of marriage!"

She laughed and said, "He knows how it works. He pays the bills, and I run the house." She continued to laugh. Then she confessed, "We have become friends."

Smiling, I looked at him and said, "Did you tell her what your response was?"

He said, "See, you are trying to get me in trouble," and we all laughed.

Leigh Howlett and Adam De La Roche Souvestre,
partners for eleven years — Something About Us

SOMETIMES, YOU HAVE TO LET THEM HAVE IT

I tended to a patient who had a fainting episode. He was sixty-three years old. His wife was so mad at him because she didn't think he was taking good care of himself. They had been married for **thirty-five years**. I asked him about those thirty-five years and how that came about.

He pointed to his wife and said, "That's my 'Road Dog.' All I have is her and Jesus."

She quipped, "Thirty-five years, lots of prayers and genuine love."

I knew she wanted to "let him have it," but she was attempting to maintain her composure, I let him have it on her behalf. I said to him, "I am sure your 'Road Dog' would like you to be around for thirty-five more years. That means you should be more active in your healthcare."

With a slight smile, his wife appreciatively looked at me and winked.

PRAYER AND PROMISES

The seventy-seven-year-old patient I went to see was found at home with very low blood sugar. Her seventy-eight-year-old husband came with her to the ER. They had been married for **fifty-two years.**

As I stood at the foot of the bed, I asked, "How did you manage fifty-two years?"

She shouted from the bed, "Prayer!"

He followed with, "She is right, but there are other things, such as being compassionate and understanding. We talk about everything. Communication." He exclaimed, "Oh! Remember your vows, what you promised God."

I inquired, "How did you meet?"

He replied, "She was married before, and I met her through her children." With a smile, he added, "otherwise, she would have walked right past me."

REMINISCES OF A HAPPY MARRIAGE

I had a patient who was 100 years young! She stood five feet three inches, with a beautiful brown smooth complexion, very few wrinkles, and wore eyeglasses. She had been married for **forty-one years** to her late husband.

She said, "I loved him, and he loved me too, I think." She laughed.

Her daughter was at her bedside and laughed with her mom.

She continued, "I enjoyed being married, but I didn't remarry. One marriage was enough. I enjoyed it while it lasted," and she laughed again. She wistfully said, with a faraway look, "We used to love walking outside." She added, "We had five children and have eight grandkids."

BE CREATIVE IN DIRECTING

My patient was not the interviewee. Rather, my conversation about longevity was with the patient's father, a very regal gentleman who possessed a very tailored style. He was visiting his son, and in exchange, he mentioned he was a detective in Chicago and had been married for **sixty-six years**.

"Wow!" I exclaimed as I raised my eyebrows. "Congratulations!"

He said, "After sixty-six years, you learn how to say 'Yes!' You also learn how to duck and stay clear of the line of fire that might be aimed in your direction, even if it is not aimed at you. You need to be the captain at the helm," he explained, "specifically directing your wife without her realizing it." He raised both hands as if he was about to direct a choir and candidly added, "Be creative in love."

Sade's song, *Smooth Operator*, came to mind as I smiled while listening to him. I would have loved the opportunity to chat with his wife and get her response.

GIVE AND TAKE GOES BOTH WAYS

"**I** am having my first nosebleed ever," said the fifty-six-year-old woman. "I am shocked at the amount of bleeding that comes from a small space as your nose!"

Her husband of **twenty-five years** accompanied her.

I looked at him and inquired, "How did you make it to twenty-five years?"

He laughed and simultaneously shook his head, he said, "Give and take."

She responded, "Yep! Give and take on both persons' part."

SOMETIMES YOU WON'T KNOW WHY

The patient lying in bed was looking up at his wife. "She has been by his side for sixty-three years," he declared.

I responded, "That is fantastic! **Sixty-three years**! That's impressive!"

She told me, "You need to have a sense of humor, the ability to hang in there, and patience." She enthusiastically added, "And have lots of fun together!"

I looked in his direction, and he said, "I don't know," and then laughed.

As she continued to speak, he shook his head and repeated, "I don't know," as he laughed some more.

TRUST THE LORD

When I walked into the room, an eighty-nine-year-old woman hunched over, rubbing her knee. She was in the ER with knee pain and swelling.

She said she had been married for **forty-eight years**, so I inquired, "What is your secret for forty-eight years?"

She pondered the question for a minute and replied, "I don't know if there was any secret." She continued to share, "There are some good men, and some bad ones. I picked a good one. I'm not saying that everything was a bed of roses. We have our share of ups and downs." She said, "We had some good times," nodding her head. Furthermore, you have to trust the Lord." She repeated, "Yes, trust the Lord."

"And now these three remain; Faith, Hope, and Love. But the greatest of these is Love."

— *1 Corinthians 13: 13*

MATES MAKES A DIFFERENCE

This is a tale of three mates. A seventy-year-old guy came to the ER with two of his best mates. He'd been on a tin roof removing nails and, not wearing gloves, had cut his finger. The patient had been married **thirty-four years**, and this was his third marriage. The second guy had been married for thirty-seven years and the third friend, twenty-two years.

I asked my patient about his thirty-four years of longevity.

As he looked from one friend to the other, he said, "The key is to do what your wife says, but we are not going to tell her about this trip to the Emergency Room."

One of his mates said, "Yeah! We know how she will react." They all laughed as they nodded their heads in agreement.

The youngest of the three, married twenty-two years, said, "You need patience. Think about what you don't like about the person, and if you can live with that, you are good." He continued, "You can't change people, although my wife took my necklace and made it a chokehold. She slowed me down big time."

They all laughed heartily.

The mate who had been married thirty-seven years said, "Yep! Do what the wife says. Spend time together but spend time apart also." As he pointed to his friends, he said, "We all spend time together."

The youngest of the three interjected, "But you can't be partying when you spend time apart."

Looking at them, I could feel the genuine friendship and love they had for each other.

I wondered why a seventy-year-old man would be doing demolition on a tin rooftop without gloves. Not thinking—eh!

LET EACH OTHER PLAY

Motocross is popular here in New Zealand, and this was the third guy over seventy who I had seen as a patient from an injury due to that sport.

My patient had been married to his wife for **forty-two years**.

He said, "She lets me have my toys—motorbikes, guns, etc.—and I let her have her jewelry, diamonds to be exact. We love to travel. We went to America and loved it, so we are going back in a few months."

His wife smiled. Then she said, "The secret is that he married well," and she threw her head back and laughed. "Really, I don't know if there is a secret," she said. "We travel a lot. We both have four brothers, and they all have been married for more than forty years. People don't do that anymore."

BE READY FOR CHANGE

I had a seventy-five-year-old patient from Gambia who was visiting one of his twelve children. He had been married for **forty year**s.

He told me, "You marry for better or worse, for richer or poorer. You have to accept whatever comes because tomorrow is another day. When I am poor today, tomorrow, I may be rich. When I am rich today, I may be poor tomorrow. You must accept it."

HAVE FAITH AND COMMITMENT

As I pulled the exam room curtains back, there was a woman who looked fiery red from an all-over-body rash. I treated her symptoms and told her she needed to stay for a while of observation.

I looked at her husband and asked, "Do you mind if I ask how long you have been married?"

He stated matter-of-factly, "We have been married for **forty-one years** of bliss."

She interjected, "Well, it hasn't all been bliss."

He said, "To have longevity, you need perseverance, commitment, and have individual interests and faith. Most of all, faith." As he spoke, she nodded her head in affirmation.

She echoed her husband and said, "Commitment. You need to have commitment."

He told me they had three sons and four and 'three-quarter' grandchildren. He smiled and explained, "Our daughter-in-law is having a baby soon."

TIME PASSES WHEN YOU HAVE FUN

I had a gentleman who came in with epigastric and left side pain. The pain was located directly in that little spot at the top of your stomach where you point to when you think you have indigestion. He had been feeling unwell for a week. He didn't want to come to the ER, but his wife made him come. It turned out that he had pneumonia.

As I peered in her direction, she said to him, "See why I made you come to see the doctor?"

Then I asked, "How long have you been the boss?"

She replied, "We have been married for **fifty years**."

"Amazing," I said, "and how did you make it to fifty years?"

As she smiled and shook her head simultaneously, she admitted, "I don't know." With relative surprise, she echoed, "Fifty years! That's a long time!"

Her husband started laughing and gleefully expressed, "We had fun!"

She smiled and nodded in agreement.

EVERYONE HAS THEIR MOMENTS

I was speaking with an older gentleman who fell off a stool and hit his head. His wife was concerned and called the paramedics immediately. He was not happy about all the fuss, despite having a huge scalp wound. He boasted that his wife had been by his side for **fifty-four-and-a-half years**.

He said, "It is because I know how to say, 'Yes, dear.'"

She remarked, "Tolerance, that is what it is." She continued, "We are still talking. We have had a few 'trips,' but we are still here."

"Congratulations," I expressed. "Both of you are to be commended!"

"Yes," she said, "I guess it is quite a long time, isn't it?"

I responded, "It certainly is. People break up these days after two or three years."

She agreed and added, "That's because they don't talk."

Her husband interjected, "We have had our moments lately, haven't we, dear."

THE RIGHT THING OR
THE RIGHT WOMAN?

One evening, a dairy farmer came to the ER because of back pain. His daughter forced him to come in. If you know anything about dairy farmers, they don't go to see the doctor easily for anything, not even if they cut off a finger. (Yes, that did happen!) Further, if you saw a dairy farmer lying on one of your ER gurneys, you would always be on high alert because whatever they came in for is the 'real deal.' His daughter looked at him sternly, and she shook her head at his stubbornness.

He and his wife had been married for **thirty-nine years**, and their fortieth wedding anniversary was two weeks away.

He started saying, "The secret to longevity is doing the right thing—"

Before he finished expressing his response, his wife touted, "He married the *right* woman."

She then sat up straighter and looked pleased with herself.

HOLDING IT IN

Anaphylaxis, a highly severe form of an allergic reaction, can be scary, even for a doctor. A call came over the hospital radio that a sixty-two-year-old male patient had an anaphylactic reaction. When the patient reached the ER via the paramedics, he had not improved much, but he was not worse either. We worked quickly to give him medications to help ease his symptoms.

He said that he and his wife were going on vacation for their **fortieth wedding anniversary** and they decided to have an impromptu party. Someone suggested to his wife to put on her wedding gown during the party. She thought it was silly, but she got her gown and put it on anyway.

I thought *I was astonished she still had the dress some forty years later.* She was surprised that she could still fit into it. The ring bearer, who was two years old when they got married, was at the party. This time, he walked her down a make-believe aisle. Her granddaughter carried her train.

Regarding longevity, she said, "During the forty years, you take it all in. You do what you can and don't say much." She let out a huge, long, drawn-out sigh and lamented, "I usually have a rumbling in my stomach from holding things inside. Then I cry, and everything is all right."

His thoughts on longevity were, "I guess I married the right woman."

She remarked, "People don't stay married for long anymore."

He chimed in, "Not the young ones anyway."

LAST WORDS ON A LONG MARRIAGE

When I saw the ECG (heart tracing) of the eighty-eight-year-old man who collapsed at home, I knew things were not good. He had a heart attack. His troponin level (the enzymes that tell us about the heart muscle) was 6,500. Less than 15 is normal at our hospital. I spoke with him about his ECG, lab results, and what needed to be done moving forward. While discussing the diagnosis and next steps, I learned a little more about the couple who had been married for **sixty-two years**.

She said, "Things have been great up until this last week. He has been keeping me up at night because he was not feeling like himself." She smiled and said, "I just do what I am told."

He laughed and said, "You mean, how did I survive her?" Then he laughed even more. He pondered and said, "I don't know if there is a secret. Just stay together."

He died a day later. One of the nurses told me that his wife had come back to the ER to look for me because she wanted to thank me for taking good care of her husband.

HOW TO STAY YOUNG
AND OTHER THINGS

An eighty-two-year-old gentleman came in with chest pain. After examining him, completing tests and x-rays, he was ready to be discharged home.

"After **fifty-four years** of marriage," he said, "I don't think there is a secret. There is no one thing."

His wife stated, "You have to take it all, the good with the bad." She continued, "We have three boys and ten grandkids. We go to a lot of their games, and it keeps us young."

KEEP ON TALKING, EVEN WHEN YOU CAN NO LONGER DANCE

The chief complaint on the patient's chart, the reason this patient came to the ER was due to a cough and chronic sinus problems. He spoke with me, expressing that he felt as if he could not shake "it," whatever "it" was. "This is keeping me up at night," he said.

I looked toward his wife, and I asked how many years they had been married. In a somber tone, she replied, "Married for **forty-nine years**."

"How did you manage forty-nine years?" I asked her.

As she opened her mouth to speak, with passion her husband interjected, "Oh! Communication."

She pointed in his direction as she tilted her head, reinforced his thoughts, and said, "That's it. You have to communicate. You have to talk, talk, talk."

He said, "We discuss everything. We talk about everything."

She told me that she could speak to her friends about a specific topic, then later, she would speak to their partner about the same thing. She discovered that her friends never discussed that subject with their partners. "We constantly talk," she repeated.

He revealed later that he used to power lift. "Back then, I could lift three times my weight," he said with pride.

I smiled on a sly because it begged the question that I had to ask, "Are you still lifting up your wife?"

He emphatically declared, "Oh, no, no, no!"
She blushed, chuckled, and said, "Those days are long gone."

"To keep your marriage brimming,
With love in the wedding cup,
Whenever you're wrong, admit it;
Whenever you're right, shut up."

— Ogden Nash

TIME FLIES BY

I had the sweetest eighty-two-year-old lady who needed sutures. As she attempted to get to a ringing phone, she fell, hitting her head on something. Her husband was at her bedside, holding her hand as I sutured her scalp wound. I inquired how long they had been holding hands.

He said, "For **fifty years**. We celebrated fifty years about three months ago, right, honey?"

"Yes!" she replied.

I asked, "How has fifty years been?"

She lovingly gazed at him and stated, "It's been fifty years, but it doesn't seem like it's been that long. The time went so fast."

"Yes," he responded in his kiwi accent. (I *love* the New Zealand accent.) "It's been fifty years. Yes, it doesn't seem that it has been fifty years at all," he said in agreement.

I watched as they chatted back and forth, and it appeared as if the question that I asked was a catalyst for making them focus on the fact that fifty years had genuinely gone. I never got an answer about the longevity of their marriage. It was sweet to witness the couple's genuine awe of their achievement of fifty years of marriage, and rightfully so. Then I thought, *maybe I did get my answer.*

BE KIND, DON'T ARGUE

"I think I may be having a stroke," the eighty-two-year-old man said to me. "All of a sudden, things went numb on my right side, and I couldn't move my arm too well." He lifted his right arm and said, "I couldn't do this about three hours ago."

I examined him, ordered some tests and blood work.

His wife stated, "I told him to take an aspirin."

He informed me, "That's for your heart, dear."

"However, he didn't take it." She remarked, "Oh well!"

I asked if they minded if I inquired how long they had been together.

As she looked toward her husband, she said, "Honey, it's been **thirty-five years**, right?" Then she looked at me and added, "We just celebrated our son's thirtieth birthday."

He replied, "Yes."

"What has been the catalyst to thirty-five years," I asked.

He proclaimed, "We never have had an argument."

As she laughed, she revealed, "His last marriage was thirty-eight years, and I told him that I was determined to exceed that duration."

I didn't ask what happened to his first wife, whether she had died or they got divorced.

SOMETIMES YOUR OTHER
HALF WON'T LISTEN

I picked up the chart to see my next patient, and the reason for the visit was that the patient had fallen off his motorcycle. I walked into the room. There sat a seventy-two-year-old man in bed, with his wife sitting on a chair toward the foot of the gurney. I could already discern that she was not pleased with him. He was doing motocross, went over a jump, and you know the rest.

They had been married **forty-nine years**. On the question of longevity, she replied first.

She said, "He is a lovely person, and he likes my cooking."

He looked up from the gurney and said, "What did she say?"

I told him, "She said, 'You like her cooking.'"

"Well, okay," he said.

Then she stated in a very matter-of-fact tone, "Apparently, we have a problem with communication at the moment. I told him to stay off that bike."

DO THE HARD WORK

"**M**y right hip, Doc, that's my problem. I fell," said the eighty-two-year-old man.

Fortunately, he had not broken his hip. I was glad since hip fractures and the elderly do not mix well. For that matter, hip fractures don't mix well with anyone particularly the elderly.

He and his wife married **sixty-four years** ago.

He said, "She is a *good* woman," with a noticeable emphasis on good. "We have five children," he informed me. "This is our eldest daughter," pointing to the other woman standing beside his wife.

His wife's reply was succinct, "Worn out, woman now."

BE FRIENDS FIRST

The male patient, sixty-one years of age, had an unconscious collapse. His blood sugar level had fallen very low, and he had fainted. The paramedics, who brought him into the ER, gave him some glucose (sugar) on site. Consequently, he was conscious and doing much better by the time I saw him.

He told me he had been married for **thirty-five years**.

He said, "She's the boss," with a jovial laugh as he lay in bed. Then he stated, "We were friends before we were married. We knew each other five years before she asked me to marry her."

I felt compelled to ask, "Did she ask you to marry her?"

As he broadly grinned with dancing eyes, he replied, "No, that's just what I tell everyone."

SEE THE FUTURE TOGETHER

An eighty-two-year-old man, without warning, passed out at home. "Scared me to death," his wife said.

"How long have you guys been married," I asked.

In unison, their reply was, "Married **fifty-nine years** and five months."

"It's give and take," she said.

I expressed, "It is a wonderful accomplishment."

He announced, "I have a lovely wife. It's been great. We have three great kids, eight grands and three great-grands."

His wife looked at him and announced, "His goal is to make it to the next year, right!"

BE HAPPY, JUST HAPPY

"**M**a'am, I need to let you know that you have had a heart attack, and we are very concerned about you," I said to the sixty-five-year-old woman on the stretcher. She looked anxiously at her husband sitting beside her. As preparations were occurring for her to go to the Cath Lab, I discovered they had been married for **forty-five years**.

He said, "We are together because we are happy." He got up from the chair, walked over to the side of the bed, and rubbed his wife's hand. He asked, "Are you happy?"

"No," she answered.

He said, "I know, but…" as his voice trailed off.

She assured him, "Yes, I know what you mean. Yes."

Then he patted her hand again.

That was the first time I heard anyone mention the word "happy." I daresay that doesn't mean that other couples were unhappy since many had the aura of happiness. This wouldn't be the last time I would hear the word "happy" included in someone's reply.

DRIVING EACH OTHER NUTS
SOMETIMES WORK

Abll my next patient could do was shake his head back and forth at his calamity because the sixty-eight-year-old gentleman had dropped a brick on his foot. He was building a brick wall for his wife's garden. He let me know that his wife was on her way to the hospital.

When his wife arrived, I inquired how long they had been married, and they told me **forty-eight years**.

His thought regarding longevity was, "You have to make each year happy." She said, "Lots of deep breaths." Then she added, "I don't drive." I asked, "How did you get here?"

"I power walked." Then she grinned and admitted, "No, I took the bus." Her husband said, "She drives me nuts."

I told him that I would give him a prescription for ice cream and his wife would be the one to get it. He wordlessly smiled, and then his wife left to get a cup of tea.

Once his cast was on, he asked, "How can I stand up and wash the dishes?"

"Oh!" I responded. "I will make the prescription to say, no dishwashing for one week, instead."

"Yes!" he laughed.

At the end of his visit, he *actually* requested his prescription for "no dishwashing." I wrote it, handed it to him, and he—in turn—gave it to his wife broadly grinning.

She read it, looked up at me, and asked, "What am *I* supposed to do?" She shook her head as she looked at her husband and laughed.

"Love is that condition in which the happiness of another person is essential to your own."

— *Robert A. Heinlein*

TAKING CARE AND TOLERANCE

I walked into the room of a seventy-nine-year-old man having an allergic reaction. I requested that he remove his shirt so that I could examine him.

His wife chuckled and said, "The female paramedic also took off his shirt." With an amused expression, she said, "Honey, every woman wants you to remove your shirt." Then she laughed again.

They had been married **fifty years**, and their fifty-first anniversary was around the corner in two months. She laughed from her belly and said, "I can't tell you how swimmingly we get along." She continued, "Fifty years. We get along, but you need to have a sense of humor." As she pointed toward his direction, she declared, "I have taken great care of him. He has never been in a hospital."

He remarked, "We tolerate each other well."

"Now that he is retired and home, we spend time in different rooms, which helps," she said. To feign revealing a secret, his wife put her hand to her mouth as she looked toward me and said, "I would sometimes send him to his mother. She lives in Wales," she said with a sly smile."

A LITTLE COMPETITION CAN
BE A GOOD THING

A charming seventy-year-old woman presented to the ER after falling outside, and a bystander called the paramedics.

She told me she had been married **forty years** and said, "The key is that he worked, and I worked. He drinks. I don't, but it's okay since I put my foot down when it's too much. He quit smoking when I quit smoking." Then she admitted, "It's a competition between us."

SECOND CHANCES

My patient, eighty-four years old, informed me that she used to be a midwife and also taught piano. She and her late husband had decided they were going overseas when they married. But she wanted to wait until she graduated with her nursing degree before she went. She said they had been married for **fifty-eight years**.

I asked how they met.

She said, "Before getting married, I had one daughter and twin boys. One of the twins died about six years of age. While working as a midwife, I got called in to work to help with a patient. The patient's husband came to see his wife, but she had died." She continued, "I spoke with him to let him know I had been through a similar event. He was grateful for my empathy and our talk. Later, he came back to express, thank you."

She shared, "After a while, we married and had three children."

WORK TOGETHER

I picked up a chart before going to see a seventy-six-year-old woman with a head injury. A falling clothesline hit her.

As she explained what had happened, she looked toward her husband. "He didn't lock the bar, so it fell on top of my head as I was hanging the clothes." She confessed, "I swore a lot," and for emphasis, she balled her hand into a fist and shook it at him.

They told me they had been married for **fifty-six years**. I asked, "How have you made it fifty-six years?"

He told me, "Be happy." He expounded by saying, "Well, you won't be happy all the time, but don't be unhappy all the time. I've always said, 'If you are mad, talk about it before going to bed. If you don't and sleep on it, then it will fester.'"

"What he said is right," she interjected. She continued, "He has always said that. Work together. We've had ups and downs, and we lost a son."

He voiced with a hint of admiration and pride, "My parents were married for seventy years. They were well into their nineties."

I winked at her and offered, "Should I write a prescription that says you get anything you want for one week?"

With a smile, her husband quickly replied, "Well, she *always* gets what she wants." Then he admitted, "Well, most of the time."

BE PLAYFUL WITH EACH OTHER

An eighty-one-year-old gentleman with chest pain sat up in bed as his wife held his hand in the room. His EKG, the electronic tracing of his heart, showed signs of a heart attack. He was attended to promptly. He and his wife of **fifty-four years** had known each other three years before he asked her to marry him.

"I was waiting for her to ask me," he said with an amused expression.

She laughed and said, "You are terrible." She looked back at me and shared, "We were sitting in the movie theater, and he said, 'Have you seen a ring you like?'"

Jesting, I inquired, "Is that really how he proposed to you?"

She replied, "Yes, no getting on his knee or anything."

Feigning defensiveness, he claimed, "It's the marriage, not the words, right!" After pausing for a moment, he said in a serious tone, "We both came from broken homes."

The nurse entered the room. As he was about to be wheeled to the Cardiac Unit, he looked at his wife and teased, "Do you want to ride in the bed with me," and laughed.

"No," she said as she shook her head.

The nurse remarked, "We need to watch these two," as she smiled at their banter.

They were lively with each other. It made my heart feel light, and I had the biggest smile. I thought *this is what has helped carry this couple through fifty-four years.*

BE SUPPORTED BY GOD

They were both from farming families, and this couple had their own farm. After **forty-two years** of marriage, they were still going strong, and their farm.

"Wow!" I exclaimed and extended a sincere, "Congratulations!"

"Yeah, wow," she echoed. The wife further commented, "It hasn't always been easy. God is the reason why we are still together. We have to be willing to do God's work and be diligent. You can't get personal, and God has to be in the center. When things get tough, I say, 'Remember your promise to God.' He guides me. God is the reason."

Amen to that!

KNOW WHEN YOU'RE BLESSED

I pulled back the exam room curtain and saw an eighty-one-year-old man holding his nose with his head tipped back. He said that he could not get his nose to stop bleeding this time around. His wife of **forty-eight years** was beside him. After treating him, I asked the couple the question of longevity.

His wife said, "We've had our ups and downs. I have a deep faith, and that's been a great help." She volunteered, "we have six children."

He asserted, "We are blessed."

DO THE WORTHWHILE WORK

As I walked into the room, I could tell the man lying in bed was quite unwell. With haste, I attended to him. He and his wife had been married for **forty-five years**.

On the question of their longevity, she said, "He is very patient," as she gently rubbed his hand. She looked up and said, "Be happy, work hard. It's a lot of work," she emphasized.

Being quite ill, her husband couldn't answer, but he did tell me how many years they had been married.

"Love; a fruit always in season."

— Mother Theresa

ONE PAGE SOMETIMES MAKES
THE BEST BOOK

As I entered the room, the patient's husband blurted out, "She gave us quite a scare," referring to his sixty-eight-year-old wife, who had collapsed earlier. As part of her mental status exam, I asked her how long she had been married.

She replied, "**Forty-eight years**," as she glanced toward her husband.

"Terrific! And who is that?" I said, pointing to her husband.

She said, "That's the man I've been married to, my husband."

"What is his name?" I asked.

She told me, beaming.

I looked at him and then looked at her and said, "Are you going to write a book?"

He spoke up fast, "It would be a short book, one page," he said. "Marriage is easy," as he burst out into laughter. "Yes, that's right."

I raised my eyebrows at him and said, "Really?"

After attending to his wife and getting her paperwork ready for discharge, I looked at him and said, "One page, huh," and then I burst out laughing.

He looked at me and said, "What are you worried about? What's the issue? One page," he repeated as he held up one finger. "Marriage is easy," he said, as he doe-ed over his wife of forty-eight years.

ENJOY YOUR TIME TOGETHER

A seventy-eight-year-old man presented with vomiting and weakness. He had been unwell for several days. He and his wife had tried what they could to help him feel better. They were on vacation, and as they were driving home, he got ill.

I looked at him and said, "Who is the better driver?"

He said, "Don't look at me," and nodded toward his wife.

I said, "Oh," and proceeded to ask how long they had been married.

"**Sixty-one years**," they said in unison.

"And how did you make it to sixty-one years?" I asked.

She stated, "We've had a good life."

He agreed, "We've had a good life. Three great daughters," he added.

He continued, "We traveled a lot, we took a lot of vacations," shaking his head in the affirmative.

As she sat there with her hands between her knees as if she was warming them, she said again, "We had a good life, and we have enjoyed our time together."

EIGHTY YEARS OF MARRIAGE

O ne day while listening to NPR WABE 90.1 (an Atlanta, GA public radio station), they were celebrating a couple who had reached a vast milestone wedding anniversary. I didn't hear the radio broadcast from the beginning, so I don't have many particulars, but I tuned in to catch the words, "… this couple is celebrating their **eightieth wedding anniversary**."

Sweet Jesus. I was floored, thinking, *is that really possible? Shut the front door! Eighty years of living with the same person! Wow! did they get married at birth! I* shook my head. I couldn't fathom this. *Who stays together for eighty years?! I was astounded — what a testament of longevity.*

THE TIME JUST GOES BY

My patient was a seventy-three-year-old gentleman in one of the resuscitation bays with chest pain. His wife was sitting in the chair with a lot of concern and amusement. The patient was doing okay, although concerned about the chest pain he was experiencing.

To the question of how long they have been wedded.

"**Fifty-two years**," she said while nodding in the affirmative.

He looked at me and said, "It feels like sixty-two," and laughed.

She raised one eyebrow and said, "Okay now."

I looked back at him and ran my finger horizontally across my neck and smiled.

"How did you manage fifty-two years?" I asked no one in particular.

She answered, "The time just goes by."

CHASING LOVE

A ninety-year-old man was feeling unwell, and his wife called the paramedics to bring him to the hospital.

"Reluctantly, he came," she said to me.

They had been together for **sixty-nine years**. The gentleman's clarity at ninety was terrific. He could tell me the name of all his medications, which weren't many, and he proceeded to give me his unsolicited opinion of the then forty-fifth USA President… whom he wasn't impressed with.

I ask his wife, "Did you make him chase you long?"

She blushed and said, "No, it was a short time before we decided we wanted to be married."

And she proceeded to tell me how they met.

"We met in the stairwell in college. I was eighteen, and he was twenty-one. Two weeks later, he asked me to go home to meet his parents. I told him, 'I can't go home with you to meet your parents.' So, he asked a friend of his to come along, and we both met his parents. Afterwards, he asked me to marry him, and two years later, we got married."

I ask, "What has kept you together for sixty-nine years?"

She looked longing at him and said, "We just loved each other."

He smiled and stuck out his chest.

I teased him and said, "You were quick on the draw. You weren't letting her get away, were you?"

He responded, "When you see perfection, you grab it."

Smooth! I thought to myself. I was inspired by looking at the two of them. I thought to myself, *sixty-nine years, that's more years than I have been alive.*

BE GRATEFUL FOR THE BEST YEARS

The nurse called me over to look at an ECG tracing of a ninety-two-year-old lady. She was lying in bed and asked if she could have a cup of tea. She was having chest pain. She apologized for taking valuable time by coming to the hospital because the pain had subsided. I assured her that she was in the right place and had done the right thing by pushing her panic button.

She was a widow, lived alone, and had three children.

I asked her how long she had been married?

She answered, "We were married for **fifty-two years**," before adding, "and we had three beautiful children."

I tell her, "That was a long time to be married. My hat is off to you both."

Her reply was, "Those were the best years of my life." Tears began to well up in the corners of her eyes. I held her tiny hand. Her husband died several years ago. She spoke so fondly of him and her children.

She looked up at me from the bed and said, "Thank you for listening."

I smiled at her and said, "Ah, no worries."

"A successful marriage requires falling in love many times, always with the same person."

— Mignon McLaughlin

WORK THINGS OUT

The room spinning, you're spinning. No one likes the feeling of dizziness. The sixty-nine-year-old lady lying on the bed with the lights off was unhappy about her current state of being. Her husband told her that she would feel better soon—now that she was at the hospital.

They tell me they have been married **forty-eight years**. "What helped you to get to forty-eight years?" I asked.

"We had known each other a year or two," he stated as he smiled and looked endearing toward his wife. He said, "You have to be committed to working it out. She doesn't like climbing on things, but I have gotten her to walk across rope bridges a hundred feet up. My friends ask how I do it." His grin widened. "We take a vacation every year, sometimes twice a year."

She looked at him and said, "I think tolerance is key. You have to work things out."

"Yes," he said. "The longer you are together, the luckier you are. We have been very lucky."

"Congratulations," I said. "You should write a book."

She replied, "Yes, young people leave for any little thing. They get mad, argue, and leave."

Her husband shared, "We both still work. She hardly ever goes to the doctor. So when she goes down, I get concerned."

GROW ROOTS TOGETHER

I picked up the chart of the next person to see. Chest pain for one week was the history written on the chart. Turns out, this eighty-year-old man had signs of a heart attack, based on his tests.

His wife looked anxiously at him. They have been married for **fifty-eight years**. Four children and three grandchildren.

I asked about their fifty-eight years of marriage.

"We came to New Zealand as immigrants," she said, "through the Panama Canal. Six weeks on the boat. We were young, twenty-one and twenty-two. We didn't know any better. We had no family here. You tough it out. There was nowhere for me to run."

"You work together," he said. "We didn't know a soul here."

I looked at his wife and asked if she had ever cut his hair. They both laughed.

"Yes," she said.

He was still laughing as he told me the story of her cutting his hair for the first time.

He said, "she cut me bald down the center. We thought it was a number four-blade, but it was a number two blade. She didn't test it on the back of my hair, first."

She interjected, "I was panicking, but he told me it didn't matter. I was in tears," she said.

He was still laughing and said, "I didn't care. We were going on vacation."

Rhonda and Lance Locher, married eighteen years
— Have Faith in God

LOVE THE BONDS THAT LAST

I don't recall the circumstances that brought this patient to the Emergency Department, but she and her husband had been married for **fifty-five years**.

She said, "We have a strong bond. We have always tried to work together. Our youngest is a special needs child. I think that either brings you together or splits you up. It brought us together."

Her husband sat in the chair near the head of the bed, nodding in agreement.

DO WELL TOGETHER

My patient is ninety-six and looking pretty spry for her age, but she is having an issue with bleeding. Her ninety-three-year-old husband was at her side as he has been for **sixty-three years** of marriage. I thought, *holy moly! Sixty-three years!*

"Tell me the key to sixty-three years of being with the same person."

"I don't know," he said, "Good family, I guess."

"We have nineteen great-grands." She smiled. "Haven't we done well!"

A RING FOR LIFE

The eighty-three-year-old patient was in the ER because he had something stuck in his throat. Her daughter and husband were at the bedside.

As we chatted, the daughter mentioned her parents had been married for sixty-two years.

"No," her dad corrected. "**Sixty-one years**.

"Sixty-one years," I echoed.

"Yes! Don't you see my hair?" he said, pointing to his head. His hair was totally white but still covered his entire head. He laughed so hard.

I also laughed as I looked toward his wife and asked how she got to sixty-one years.

She said, "Do well and get a big ring." She held her hand out for me to see. It was a stunning silver ring (maybe platinum) with a mesh look with beautiful diamonds.

He beamed as he said, "We have four beautiful daughters. You couldn't ask for better girls." His daughter was in the amen corner in agreement.

His wife stated, "He told me no more rings. He said the next ring I get will be a nose ring."

Everyone in the room laughed.

DO IT FOR LOVE

"Feeling unwell" was all that the patient stated on the chart for the ER visit. In America, "feeling unwell" is generally not a standalone chief complaint written on a chart. In New Zealand, I soon learned that it was pretty commonplace to answer "feeling unwell" as the reason for a patient's visit. After taking a history from my ninety-year-old patient to find out why he felt unwell, I proceeded to do tests and order x-rays. He required admission to the hospital.

His wife of **fifty-nine years** was sitting on the opposite side of the bed from where I was standing. She had short silvery hair; it fit her very nicely. He said they had been married fifty-seven years, but she quickly corrected him.

Their daughter was sitting in a chair next to where I was standing.

I looked at the patient's wife and asked what the secret to fifty-nine years was.

Before she could answer, her daughter sighed and stated, "It was very unromantic. He asked her to type up his records. He thought she did a good job, so he married her."

His wife added, "We were married three months after we met."

He explained, "It was after the war. I had just done my last tour of duty."

"How did you get to fifty-nine years?" I asked.

"Lots of tolerance," he said. "You can't take on every challenge. If you don't agree, ask yourself, is it true. 'To thine own self be true,'" as Shakespeare said.

"Yes, lots of tolerance," she agreed. She continued to tell the story of her long-time friend. "A friend of mine is a counselor and has been married for forty-six years. Someone asked her in forty-six years whether she ever thought about divorce. 'Divorce,' she said. 'Never! Murder often!'" Then she smiled at me and shook her head in the affirmative.

I smiled back, understanding what she meant.

"Did he pay you to type the reports?" I asked.

"No," she answered. "I did it for love." Then she pondered for a minute and said, "Yes! I think he did pay me, oh, it's been so long I can't remember," she laughed.

ENJOY THE SAME FACE EVERY DAY

One of the paramedics brought in a seventy-eight-year-old gentleman who had collapsed at home. The patient had no recall of what had happened to him. They wheeled him into one of the critical care areas of the ER. His wife wasn't far behind, the medic informed us.

When she arrived she sat on the chair close to the gurney. The patient was very stoic and kept repeating that he was alright.

I learned they were from Samoa. I was in the midst of learning a few phrases in Samoan, but thought I wouldn't torture him with my newbie level of their language. However, I did greet him with *"Talofa, oa mai oe"* (the traditional greeting for hello, how are you). He told me that he and his wife had been married for **forty-nine years**.

His wife was sitting with her legs crossed, elbow on her thigh, with her chin planted in the palm of her left hand. She raised her eyebrows ever so slightly, and with pursed lips, she said, "Yes, forty-nine years next month, looking at the same face."

I asked her how did they get to forty-nine years?

She replied, "We have a happy marriage. We have no problems."

LESSONS IN LOVE

"**I** think I am in the wrong room," I said to the patient as I entered. This chart says you are ninety-three years old.

His smile covered his face, and he said, "That's right, and now I feel every year of it."

But the years had been kind to him, and he had a youthful appearance. He had fallen and injured his left shoulder. As we chatted, he told me he had been married for **sixty years**. "And we are still in love!" he said.

"What kept you together for sixty years," I inquired?

He answered, "I married a lovely woman. She is eight years younger than me. How she picked me up off the floor, I don't know." (He referred to the fall he had earlier that landed him in the ER.) "She was a wonderful mother, and she was always fit. She was a contortionist, you know. She taught my daughter how to dance."

"Life is a romantic business, but you have to make the romance."

— *Oliver Wendell Holmes*

LOVE EACH OTHER'S LOVELINESS

My seventy-three-year-old female patient said, "Doctor, things just aren't moving, and it's been several days now."

I replied, "Yes, that can cause you to feel quite uncomfortable."

Her husband was sitting near the foot of the bed.

She said they had been married for **forty-eight years**. Then she said, "Really, we are two months shy of forty-eight years."

"Well done," I told her. "I am giving you the last two months," and chuckled. "How did you make it to forty-eight years?"

He said, "*Lovely* woman."

She said, "*Lovely* man."

He then responded, "I had to get it in first," as he laughed. Then he looked at me and announced, "It's work."

She chimed in, "Yes, all relationships take work."

YOU HAVE TO LAUGH A LOT

As I walked into the room, my eighty-eight-year-old patient was looking at her foot. She had fallen and injured her ankle, which was swollen on one side. She was not the least bit amused with herself. She told me that she and hubby have been together for **sixty-one years**.

"Stop it! Sixty-one years. How did you manage that feat?" I asked.

They grabbed each other's hands, and she said, "We still love each other." She continued, "You have to laugh a lot—"

Her husband chimed in, saying, "Lots of understanding." He smiled in her direction and repeated, "We still love each other. We have kids, grandkids, and great-grandkids."

APPRECIATE A JOB WELL DONE

An eighty-year-old woman came to the ED after having a conscious collapse. She said she had been married for fifty-seven years.

Her husband interjected, "No, **fifty-eight years**."

"Oh yes," she said, "Fifty-eight years."

"What has been the glue to make fifty-seven years, oops fifty-eight years possible?" I inquired.

She smiled at me and said, "You just have to work with each other."

He looked at me with a sly sideways grin and said, "She's done quite well, hasn't she?"

I looked at his wife, and we both smiled.

DON'T GO ANYWHERE

When I entered the examination room, the seventy-one-year-old patient lying on the bed looked as though she was asleep. She had a bad bout of what she thought was gastro, a stomach bug. She felt weak and tired. But she opened her eyes as she heard me speaking to her husband.

He told me they had been together **fifty-one years**.

"To last this long," she said, "You have a good go round" as she smiled and then broke out into a loud laugh. "Isn't that right?" She said, looking at her husband.

He replied, "You build trust, love, and you learn to disagree. You have two people from different families, so you have to learn to disagree."

She told me, "He was in the military, and he left me—"

He finished the story and said, "Yes, and when I got back, she said, 'You are not going anywhere else without me.'"

"Smart woman," I whispered in her direction, knowing he could hear me.

I asked, "Who is the better driver?"

She said, "I never learned to drive. We are still in love."

As she spoke, her husband had a proud look on his face.

WORK TOGETHER TO FIND COMPROMISE AND FORGIVENESS

"It's likely just indigestion," my eighty-eight-year-old patient said to me as I attempted to silence the cardiac monitor alarm. I had to push the buttons several times before the alarms would turn off. As I walked back toward her bed, I said, "That monitor is being stubborn."

Her husband, who was ninety years old, was sitting in a chair near her bed. He pointed toward his wife and said, "Her too," implying his wife was stubborn as well.

I pointed to his wife and asked, "Who, your wife?"

He continued to point at her as he shook his head in the affirmative.

She agreed and said, "Yes, I am stubborn."

They were two months away from celebrating **sixty-three years** of marriage. "You deserve two congratulations and a curtsey," I said.

They met while participating in a sports club. They both played basketball. I ask, "How did you two manage to get to sixty-three years?"

She spoke up first: "You have to work together, compromise, and be forgiving," she explained. You have to be willing to forgive. We all make mistakes. It's so crucial to a marriage," she said.

He said, "We loved each other, and we still do," as he looked at her in the most adoring way.

"I agree," he said, "forgiveness is important."

"We did a lot of things together," she said. "A lot of volunteer work, a lot of community work. I was the secretary of our organization until five years ago." She smiled and said, "I used to keep my hair dyed then." Her hair was a beautiful mane of silver grey all over.

YOU CAN HOLD YOUR BREATH A SHORT TIME

My seventy-seven-year-old male patient was in the ED because of right-side neck pain. He has been married for **eighteen years**. I know it is less than my twenty-five years or more criteria, but they seemed like a great couple, so who cares.

When I asked what was the key to eighteen years?

He replied, "Oh no! The secret is patience," he said with emphasis.

His wife replied, "we are too old to remember," she laughed. "That's the secret."

"I am wife number six," she stated boldly. "You have to be kind and know when to back off. If you feel like things are getting too heated - back off." She further revealed, "We don't mix money. He banks at one bank, I bank at another. So, whatever I want to do with my money, I do, and whatever he wants to do with his money, he does. It won't work for everybody, but it works for us."

"Don't go to bed mad. Straighten things out. Say what you mean and let it go."

With a determined look on her face, she continued, "They say 'Life's too short.' Actually it's too long. You can hold your breath for a short while," she said, then she smiled.

I thought *that was quite a mouthful. And she was right. You can hold your breath for a short while.*

DEALING WITH LOSS

As I turned the corner of the hall, one of the nurses told me there was an eighty-one-year-old lady in cubicle seven that had suffered a conscious collapse. As I entered the room, the woman on the gurney with her arm over her forehead sighed deeply. She told me she felt dizzy, light-headed, and just had no appetite. She was not sleeping either. As I questioned her to get more information about what was going on with her, I learned her husband had died four days ago. She felt like she could not turn off her mind. They were six months away from celebrating their **sixtieth wedding anniversary**.

I told her how very sorry I was for her loss and that I knew she had lots of emotions boiling over. I said to her, "Honor your feelings, cry as many tears as you need to and however you feel is okay. God gave us tears for a reason." I also let her know that she doesn't have to be strong for anyone. That this is her time to grieve such a significant loss, and it is a process that takes time.

She replied, "I am having a difficult time sleeping because someone has slept next to me for almost sixty years." As tears rolled down her face, she looked up at me and said, "Do you want to hear this?"

I took her hand and held it in mine, "Of course I want to hear it," I said.

She gave another big sigh.

I examined her and had some tests done. I am sure the stress of losing her husband weighed in on her feelings. Losing a loved one, especially a life partner, can affect us mentally, emotionally, and physically.

Later, I ask, "How did you manage almost sixty years together?"

She said, "Someone asked us this a few years ago."

"What did you tell them," I asked.

She answered, "My husband said 'Respect. You always have respect for the other person.'"

"Yes," I replied. Then I asked, "What did you say?"

She said, "I agreed with my husband—respect." Then she smiled as she looked up at me and said, "That doesn't mean you don't get cross with them every now and then."

I smiled back, and she squeezed my hand.

"Happy is the man who finds a true friend, and far happier is he who finds that true friend in his wife."

— Franz Schubert

WHY LOOK ELSEWHERE?

Sitting on the bed was a seventy-eight-year-old woman shaking her head, still in disbelief that she had fainted. She was with her husband at a funeral, and the next thing she knew, there was a crowd of people around her. This couple married each other **fifty-six years** ago.

"How did you get here fifty-six years later?" I asked.

He replied, "It hasn't been tormenting," as he bellowed a hearty laugh.

"Don't pay him any attention," his wife responded. "He has his games, like Balls that he likes, and I have my own activities, gardening, walking, etc. Then we would meet back at home and talk about our day."

Her husband chimed in, "She would go for four-hour walks, and as she was leaving, she would say, 'You can make tea if you want.'" He laughed and confessed, "I never did."

"We have a lovely family. We are all close," she said.

He then proclaimed, "I have a great family. Why would I look for another woman?"

She looked over at him and said, "Oh! So now you tell me."

I winked at her and looked at her husband, and said, "Did she ask you to marry her" as I laughed

He said, "Almost."

She interjected and made a playful kicking motion toward him with her foot. "I had to tell him, hey hop to it."

We all laughed.

KEEPING THE LOVE WITH LOVE

"**I**'ve had a nagging headache for two days," a seventy-eight-year-old lady told me.

I questioned her about her headache and asked about other symptoms as I examined her. I wanted to check that nothing sinister was brewing.

She and her husband had been married **fifty-seven years**.

"How did you get to fifty-seven years?" I inquired.

He replied, "We are trying to make it to sixty years."

She responded, "You just stay in love. It takes you through all the bits and babies." She continued, "We met at school in the sixties. He was a schoolteacher, and back then, girls were looking for schoolteachers," she remarked, giving a hint of a smile.

As she spoke, he crossed his legs and started to swing the top one. "Yeah, I was pretty popular back then," he said with a boyish grin.

Looking at him now, I thought he was handsome, some sixty years later, so I can imagine how he must have been quite a looker in his youth, as my grandmother would say.

"Who is the better dancer?" I asked.

She quickly pointed to him, and that boyish grin was back.

Annie and Willie "Ted" Caraway, married thirty-three years — Just Being Together

KEEP THE SPARK WITH WIT AND CHARM

"You don't look too comfortable," I said as I walked into the examination room to see an eighty-five-year-old man with difficulty breathing.

He replied in a choppy sentence. "No, not... to... well."

"Let's see if we can get you feeling better," I replied. I examined him and then wrote some orders for medications to help improve his breathing.

Later, when I walked back into the room after receiving treatment, he was smiling.

He stated, "Boy, I feel a whole lot better."

"Glad to hear that," I said.

It turns out he and his wife had been married **sixty years**. "That deserves high fives, no high tens all around," I said.

With a smile on his face, he told me he managed sixty years with charm, wit, and a great smile. Then he looked and nodded in his wife's direction and said, "I'm getting a new one."

His daughter was at the bedside and replied, "You wouldn't be able to keep up," as she laughed.

His wife responded, "The years fly by, four great kids."

"Sixty years," I repeated, "Are you writing a book?" I asked him.

"Oh no! he exclaimed, "I can't do that. I imagine there would be a bit of spark if I did that," he laughed some more.

A GOOD MARRIAGE HAS MANY VIRTUES

I thought they were the cutest couple you'd ever want to meet. My patient was ninety-two years young. She stated that she was experiencing dizziness and hadn't had an appetite for the last four days or so. She was the caregiver for her husband, about the same age. They have been married for **forty-eight years**.

With a smile on her face, she said, "For forty-eight years, you put up with each other."

He chuckled and said, "Do whatever she tells you. No, really. She has a lot of good virtues," on which he expounded. "Patience— which is very important. Very encouraging—she has always been supportive of everything I do. That's important when you live in different places." He went on to explain, "I used to teach college history, and we traveled to different countries. She has exquisite taste," he boasted (referring to himself) as he showed all thirty-two's smiling.

She looked at me and said, "What did he say?"

I joked and said, "He responded you have questionable taste."

He covered his mouth, leaned over, and had a good laugh.

"Give me my hearing aids," she said. He was still laughing when he handed them to her.

ENJOY THE TIME YOU HAVE TOGETHER

The nurse looked at the wound under the patient's bandages when I entered the room. The patient was eighty-five years old and had tripped on the step. She had a huge skin tear on her leg. She was very cross with herself as she shook her head in annoyance.

Her husband of **sixty years** was sitting in the chair near her. She said they spent the first twenty years of marriage in England. She explained that over the years, "We have enjoyed life, done lots of living, and traveled."

"Yes!" He remarked, "she loves a plane. She would fly on the wing if they let her."

"Yes," she nodded, "I love a plane."

He said, "we always traveled." "Traveled while we could. Now, we can't travel."

BE A BIT STUBBORN ABOUT IT

The gentlemen I was looking after had been married for fifty-six years. I asked him how he had achieved **fifty-six years** of marriage?

He looked at me with a straight face and said, "I was too stubborn to say I made a mistake." Then he began to bellow with laughter.

His wife, sitting to his right, looked at him and rolled her eyes while shaking her head. "You can tell he loves to kid around. There is a lot of give and take."

"Yeah," he said, "I give, and she takes." He finished with a big grin on his face.

BE THERE FOR EACH OTHER

I had an eighty-two-year-old woman who presented feeling feverish. She looked as if she didn't feel well.

"I don't know what is going on with me," she said. "I just feel run down." She said she has been married for **sixty-three years**, and now her husband has dementia.

"What sustained you for sixty-three years?" I asked.

She replied, "I don't know, really. We have been pretty healthy all of our lives."

IT PAYS TO BE PICKY

My delightful patient was so upbeat despite having to come to the hospital. She was seventy-five years old, her brownish blonde hair cut just so, and owning every one of her years. She had heart palpitations and noticed some pain in her epigastric area when she bent forward.

She tells me that they are still going after **thirty-five years** of marriage. She married at the age of forty.

My mother said, "I was too picky. I just knew what I wanted, and I had a list," she proclaimed. As she moved her finger in the air, down an imaginary list. She looked at her husband and announced, "He is the gentlest man—I have ever met since my father. He is very kind." Looking in her husband's direction, she went on to say, "We don't argue, do we?"

He smiled, tilted his head ever so slightly to the side, and raised his eyebrows as he looked in my direction.

I smiled back. I understood.

STAY GROUNDED

"I don't know what happened," the seventy-two-year-old man said to me. "She claims I fainted," as he looked toward his wife of **thirty-five years**.

She explained, "As we sat on the bench in the yard looking at the pond, I had my head on his lap when he fainted. I looked up. He was slumped over and didn't respond to me for a couple of seconds."

I gathered more history before proceeding with my plan.

Later, I inquired about their thirty-five years of matrimony.

"This is both of our second marriages. You learn that you can't change people. The second time around, it's easier," he said.

"He is my rock," she said as she grabbed his hand while he lay on the gurney. "I don't know if there is a secret. He keeps me grounded. But he better not do this again," she expressed as she put her hand over her heart.

NO PLACE LIKE HOME

Ninety is the new seventy; I thought as I walked into the room to see my next patient, who had been feeling dizzy throughout the day. She didn't look anywhere close to ninety years old. Her ninety-four-year-old husband, whom she had been married to for **sixty-seven years**, was at home waiting for her.

"Sixty-seven years. That's inspiring," I said.

She met her husband during the war at the social club where she served tea.

She said, "Talking is the key to longevity. I didn't have to work. I stayed home with the kids, even when they were older."

"It's alright to disagree, but don't be disagreeable."

— Herbert Moore, Sr.

A KODAK MOMENT

If there were ever a time, I would say this is a Kodak moment, then this was it. I had a husband and wife, a ninety-three-year-old and ninety-four-year-old, respectively. They were three weeks shy of **seventy-one years** of marriage.

"What! I am speechless. Did you say seventy-one years? Oh My God!"

"Yes," she said.

They were in rooms next to each other, and they were so adorable. They were both in the ER for symptoms of pneumonia. They both had been taking antibiotic pills at home but not getting better. She took him to see their family doctor, and the family doctor sent them both to the hospital to be checked out.

"I am in awe of you," I said to her. "Seventy-one years! Congratulations! Wow! You sure about the seventy-one years?" I teased.

She smiled and thanked me.

"You know we have been blessed," she stated. "People in our day stayed together. I have looked after him pretty well—I was a nurse, you see. I heard people say they never had an argument with their partner, not sure what kind of marriage that was," she said.

"Who is the better dancer?" I cajoled.

"Oh! That was so long ago," she blushed. "We did do a bit of dancing, but neither of us was that good," she laughed.

I walked over to the next room to see her husband and said, "I asked your wife who was the better dancer. What do you think she said?"

"That she was maybe," he chuckled.

"No, she said, neither one of you was that great." He nodded his head in the affirmative and said, "She is right, you know."

"How did you make it to seventy-one years of marriage?"

He perked up and said, "She is a wonderful woman, and she takes great care of me."

I let him know that he and his wife needed admission for treatment.

"Her too," he said.

"Yes, your wife as well," I responded.

"Good," he shared, "she needs a break."

LEARN TO LOVE TOGETHER

Still trying to put the pieces together of what happened to her, my seventy-three-year-old patient had come to the hospital because she had two syncopal episodes. She and her husband were at an event. He was across the room at the time as he watched his wife begin to fall forward. She was dressed to the nines, as some say. Her short blondish-brown hair was teased just so. She possessed the most infectious smile, and it dominated the entire conversation.

Unsolicited, her husband started to speak about their longevity.

"**Fifty-two years** of marriage," her husband declared. "We have four children."

"What carried you through fifty-two years of marriage?" I asked.

He laughed and professed, "I do what I am told."

She interrupted, "You make it sound so laborious."

"No, no," he said. "I had to learn that. I was *stubborn* at first. Then, I realized happy wife, happy life," he touted.

"Yes," she chimed in. "But having your own individual interest is key also. You do things together but, you have to have your own interests as well."

He added, "You have to respect one another." She nodded in agreement. "Oh"! he said. "Now we are getting too serious here."

"We have lovely grandchildren," she boasted. "I was with my granddaughter earlier. Maybe I have been doing too much today."

BE EACH OTHER MEDALS OF HONOR

The ninety-four-year-old man sitting in front of me was feeling short of breath.

"I just haven't been breathing too well," he said.

I asked some more probing questions and treated him to help him breathe better.

"We are three months from reaching our **seventy-second wedding anniversary**," he told me.

I said, "Please take a bow, take two bows. That is amazing."

He stated, "Strong tenacity is the key to longevity," as he proceeded to laugh and cough.

His ninety-one-year-old wife replied, "I don't know, he always misbehaves," as she smiled at him.

"I got a medal for six years in the war," he announced. "I got no medal for seventy-two years of marriage." He burst out loud into laughter.

"I was the medal," his wife stated as she joined him in laughter.

RESOLVE WHATEVER'S ON THE TABLE

When I walked into the room and asked my ninety-two-year-old patient, what brought him to the hospital, he told me he was here at "her request," as he pointed to his wife of **sixty-one years**. "I told her that I was feeling faint, and then I collapsed in the garden," he explained. He had a perpetual smile and kind eyes.

His wife interjected, "He has been around for sixty-one years, and I expect him to be around for another sixty-one years." Then she looked directly at me and said, "You know how stubborn men can be."

I just smiled and nodded in agreement.

I looked from one to the other and asked, "How did you two manage sixty-one years?"

He answered instantly, "Young lady, I learned two words very earlier. They are 'yes dear.'"

He let out a roaring laugh as she picked up her walking stick and pretended to hit him, all the while laughing herself and trying to say, "That's not true."

She put down her walking stick and said, "No, really, we have never gone to bed without resolving whatever issue was on the table. We have never gone to bed mad."

He nodded in agreement and responded, "Yes, we have always talked things out." Then he looked at me with this sly grin, putting his hand up to the side of his mouth and saying in a low tone (but loud enough for his wife to hear), "She usually wins."

She picked up her walking stick again and pretended to hit him, as they both laughed.

DON'T HOLD BACK THE LAUGHTER

Sitting on the edge of the bed as I walked into the room was a seventy-seven-year-old gentleman who appeared as if he was deciding whether to stay sitting up or lie down.

He looked toward me and said, "Is this okay?" referring to himself sitting on the bed. He was in the Emergency Room because he had been coughing up blood. He continued, "I am not sure what is going on, but I am here because she thought I should come." He looked in his wife's direction. With that "I didn't want to come" look on his face.

Inside I laughed and thought, *here is another man being stubborn, as one of my previous interviewees attested.* I said, "How long has she been the boss," as I laughed.

He laughed as well, "**Fifty years**," he said proudly.

"Congratulations! That's a lot of years."

"Yes," she said. "Fifty years! It is something to celebrate. I can't believe it's been that long. I have enjoyed it, but there have been times I've wanted to just walk out. I am sure you have felt the same way, haven't you dear?" she said as she peered in her husband's direction.

He replied, "It is a lot of hard work. But us old people knew it would be." He continued, "Young people have some TV fantasy idea of marriage."

His wife nodded in agreement.

"Who is the better dancer?" I asked.

He pointed to his wife.

She laughed and said, "Yes, I like to dance." Then turning to her husband, she said, "Honey, you are a good dancer," smiling all the while. "Get a couple of drinks under your belt." Then she lets out the laughter she's holding back.

"Can I put your story in my book?"

"Yes, please do," they both said.

MAKE THE RIGHT CHOICE

The eighty-two-year-old man was lying on the bed with a smile on his face.

I introduced myself, and he said, "Hello there, how is your day going?"

"Going well," I answered. "It has just started."

He told me that he had been having pain on the right side of his stomach for a couple of days. I ask him several more questions. I told him what my plans were and the things that concerned me.

Later, he told me that he and his wife had been married for **fifty-nine years**. He further explained that they had known each other for five years before marriage. He quickly let me know that they didn't sleep together during those five years.

I smiled and nodded. I thought *only his generation would be quick to point out that fact. That is not to say that doesn't happen in today's generation.*

I asked his wife, who was sitting by the foot of the bed and had been listening as we chatted without interruption, how had she arrived at fifty-nine years.

"With great patience," she said, letting out a long deep sigh.

"And you?" I asked as I looked at her husband.

He replied with a story. "About two years ago," he said, "I was playing Balls with some mates. They asked me how long I had been married. I told them fifty-seven years, and I would marry the same woman again. They all looked at me and said, 'You would.'" He laughed.

LIVE EACH NEW DAY

Chivalry isn't dead. The eighty-seven-year-old man I was taking care of presented with blood from his left ear due to a head strike. He tried to keep his wife from falling as she reached for something above her head. He caught her, they fell, and she landed on top of him. His daughter was in attendance with him.

He told me they had been married for **sixty-seven years**. He was eighteen, and she was sixteen when they met.

"How did you come to celebrate sixty-seven years together?" I said, "That is some feat. Not to be taken lightly. My hat is off to you both, my shoes and socks too," I chuckled.

They laughed as well.

He said, "I think I've got her where I want her."

His daughter smiled and interjected, "I don't know. She was on top of you this go-round."

"You have to have tolerance and learn to give in," he explained. "When we were younger, we *never* carried things overnight. The next morning was a new day, and we started over."

"Who is the better dancer?" I inquired.

His daughter chimed in. "They were both pretty good dancers." She recalled, "When I was seventeen years old, they would drive me to school. Then they would go to dance lessons, rock 'n' roll while I was in school. They were pretty good dancers already."

PLAY TO YOUR STRENGTHS

I spoke with a couple who had been committed to each other for twenty-four years. One of the women had recently buried her mother after a long illness. Her female partner was steadily by her side. They told me they met during the Summer Olympics in Atlanta, Georgia (USA).

When I asked about the longevity of their relationship, one of the first statements from the first woman, an African American, was, "We appreciate each other's culture." (Her partner is of Japanese descent.) She continued by saying, "Communication and honesty are important. Along with respect and a sense of humor." She revealed, "I grew up in chaos, and I didn't like it."

Her partner agreed and expanded on the reason for their longevity. "We complement each other. We have different strengths, and that makes our relationship work. So many things that we do that complement each other—"

"Yes," the first woman laughed fondly and jumped back in, saying, "I clean up... But she cooks. I can only make tuna fish." They both laugh. "We have a sense of commitment and integrity."

I asked, "Who is the better driver?"

The first woman nodded toward her partner and said, "She is." Then snuck in, "Only because she has been driving longer, I didn't learn to drive until I was twenty-two."

I smiled and asked, "Who is the better dancer?"

"Me girl," stated the first woman, as she laughed. "You know that."

*Cassandra Andrews and Kathy Negrelli, partners for
twenty-four years — Play to Your Strengths*

Healthy relationships are made of communication, consideration, kindness, and plenty of give and take.

HAVE FAITH IN GOD

This couple had been together for **eighteen years** before her husband passed in 2020. The question of longevity tested their marriage straight out of the gate. Five months into their marriage, her husband developed renal failure and had a kidney transplant, and all that comes with this medical diagnosis. Years later, her husband had a massive hemorrhagic stroke (bleeding into the brain).

"He recovered, by the grace of God, she said. Then a year after recovery, he was in a very bad motor vehicle accident, and things went on a steady decline from there," she said with a heavy sigh.

I asked her how she managed those eighteen years of longevity.

She shook her head and stated, "My faith in God. We were in some of the deepest valleys. But I would try to find the joy. And with each event, I came out on the other end with my faith strengthened." She added, "I never asked why me? I believe my foundation as a child helped carry me. God determined my husband's first day and his last day," she whispered.

I asked her how they met.

She answered, "We met through mutual friends. He was a news reporter on Channel 5, which was funny because I watched Channel 7. I had never watched Channel 5 news." She laughed and continued, "He would tell people I stalked him because he was on TV. He had a great sense of humor."

"Who asked who to marry them?" I inquired.

She burst out laughing and said, "We never asked each other to marry.

We just started talking about it, and he said, 'Guess we should put it on the calendar.' We eloped, went to Jamaica, and had the locals as our witnesses. Our families found out when we showed them the wedding photo album."

STAY CLOSE

My lovely friend I spoke with has been married for **thirty-seven years**. She told me her husband was in the military when they met, and he spent a lot of time at sea. I asked her what she attributed their longevity of thirty-seven years to?

She said, "We were apart so much that we didn't take each other for granted when we shared time together."

She was a teacher and, as such, she did a lot of projects with the kids. Her husband would tell her, "I support you and your career but don't ask me to go to the craft shop and buy things [*like the other teachers' husbands*]."

She laughed as she described this and then went on to say, "We gave each other our space. We know when to give each other space and then come back together. He values family a lot." Then she laughed and said, "He also eats anything. He doesn't complain."

I asked her husband what the key to their longevity of thirty-seven years was.

"Years ago," he said, "I was in a leadership class, and our assignment was to walk into a room and command the audience's attention by telling a story that changed your life." This is the story he shared:

"I found out my sister was sick, and she lived in Puerto Rico (PR). So, I moved out of my apartment and flew back home to be with her. A good friend held on to my things for me while I was gone. When the time came for me to return to the USA, he asked me, 'Where do you want to stay?'"

I told him, "Wherever you put my things, that's where I will stay. My friend put my things in an apartment right across from where my future wife lived at the time. Because of that, I think how wonderful for me that it was her. I could have married a crazy bitch." He laughed wholeheartedly at the thought.

"I have a wonderful wife," he said with pride. He went on to say, "Relationships are give and take. Each person pisses the other person off at some point. As long as you don't piss each other off too many times. That's not good because that's when someone decides to leave." He ended, "She is the best part of me."

"Aw, that is so sweet," his wife echoed in response.

"Do you guys have a favorite song? A song that whenever you hear it, you say that's your song."

"Yes," she replied, "*Tonight, I Celebrate My Love* by Peabo Bryson and Roberta Flack." She said, "All those years, he had to leave seperated us for months, but we were always together in our hearts. I love the line in that song that says there is really no distance between us."

BRING FOOD TO THE TABLE TOGETHER

I stood at the bedside of an eighty-eight-year-old woman who was shaking her head and telling me that she felt lousy. Her blood pressure was very high at over 200. Her husband was with her, and they tell me they have been married for **sixty-seven years**.

I ask him, "Did she ask you to marry her?"

She chuckled and chimed in, "You better not answer that."

He said, "I had come to this church as a minister where she attended—

She interrupted, "I kept my eye on him," as she chuckled again.

He continued, "I wasn't there to get a girl. There were lots of girls there." He smiled and said, "She tripped me up, you see."

I replied, "So she has been tripping you up for sixty-seven years, huh?"

"Yes!" He responded as they both laughed.

"We are a match made in heaven," she said.

"That's right," he agreed.

"Who is the better dancer?" I teasingly asked.

He responded by saying, "We *never* danced."

She responded, "We weren't allowed to in those days."

He explained, "We came from strict families, and the church was very strict. So, I had to be a role model," he said as he raised his eyebrows. "It was during the war. I only went to elementary school. Very few children went to school then. We worked on the farm."

I looked at him and asked, "What do you owe the success of sixty-seven years of marriage?"

"I am well taken care of," he said in a noble manner.

"Yes!" his wife interjected. "I cook for him. We hardly argue, and we communicate."

I glanced at her husband and asked, "Do you cook?"

He laughed and then replied, "I grow all the vegetables, and beautiful meals just appear on the table."

JUST BE KIND

Early one Sunday at 6 a.m., as I entered a patient's room, I noticed the grimace on the man's face as he attempted to shift position on the uncomfortable ER gurney. This eighty-three-year-old man had tumbled down the stairs at home. He said he was getting an early start on gardening when he lost his footing, fell forward going down the stairs, and landed on his right side. After attending to him, I let him know that his x-ray showed a broken rib.

His daughter was at his bedside, shaking her head.

She pleaded, "Doctor, tell him he needs to slow down. He thinks that he can still move the way he did at twenty."

His rebuttal was, "I don't like to move slow."

I smiled at him and said, "Sir, with that broken rib, you will need to walk like an eighty-three-year-old."

He laughed as he grabbed his side and said, "Yeah, doctor, you are right."

Later, I learned that he had buried his wife two years previously. I asked him how long he had been married.

He said, "I was sixteen, and she was fourteen. What's that? Twenty years?"

"No, that's **sixty-five years**," I said. "What was your secret?" I asked.

He responded, "It was not a secret."

Then I asked again, but differently. "What was your secret to staying married for sixty-five years?"

He said, "You have to be kind and gentle. Don't hurt one another's feelings. That's real love."

I expressed my condolences for the loss of his wife. I would have loved to have known her thoughts regarding the longevity of their marriage.

SOMETHING ABOUT US

"**D**oc, you are never going to believe what happened, my part-ner was playing with our dog, and the dog's teeth caught his nose. I thought he ripped it right open." The patient sat on the gurney with expectation and was concerned about the outcome of his nose. It turns out it wasn't as bad as they thought.

I inquired about how long he and his male partner had been together. **Eleven years** said the first guy. (Yes, it's not the twenty-five-plus club, but I love their story.)

How did you meet? I asked. Again the first guy spoke up quickly.

"We were at a pizza bar, and I thought my date was 'hot.' But you know bars are dimly lit. We went outside to chat, and the streetlight hit his face. And I thought, oh no, he has red hair and freckles. I don't do freckles and red hair," he laughed heartily. He continued, "We sat and talked for about two hours over coffee, and we have been together ever since."

While he was speaking, his partner was chuckling in the background. So I asked the second guy, "How did you get to eleven years?"

He answered, "We just get each other. There was just something about him when we met. There is something about us together as well. I am impressed with what he has accomplished. We became a part of each other's development."

Once again, I spoke with the first guy and asked him about their eleven years of commitment.

He smiled and said, "He has a great butt." I laughed, and he continued, "From the moment we first met we had the same ideology, although we are totally opposite in personality. I have personnel accomplishment and he has personal accomplishments. He represented Australia in the World Games for Gymnastics. There is also the physical attraction. We've had a lot of ups and downs. We were young when we met, twenty-five and twenty-two. It was during the down times that we developed into the couple we are today. We developed and matured together. We have seen each other at our 'worst'".

"Yeah," his partner chimed in.

The first guy continued, "We've grown through those times and are still growing. When we met, he wasn't out."

Once again, the second guy spoke. "Yes, that was true," he said. "But something about him made me want to be truthful and be my authentic self. So, I did, and I told my parents."

"Who is the better dancer?" I asked.

The second guy quickly answered and said, "He is," referring to his partner.

The first guy said, "Yes, I am the better dancer, I have rhythm, and he has athleticism. He can do the worm."

We all laughed.

"Do you have a favorite song or a song that comes on, and you say that's our song?"

"Yes," answered the second guy. "We were in the Maldives a few years ago. Every time we decided to go to the beach and we're putting on sunscreen, we would hear this song called *Closer* by Chain Smoker."

I asked the first guy how he would describe his partner in three words.

He answered, "Ambitious, kind..." and then paused for a few seconds.

"I want it to count." Then in a soft voice of reflection he said "considerate".

CHERISHED WORDS

I thought it is befitting to end my last story with a couple near and dear to my heart, Aunt Enid and Uncle Roy.

One of my dearest and best friends, Dr. Sheryl Heron, and I adopted each other as sisters over thirty years ago when we met in medical school at Howard University in Washington, D.C. When she got married, her Aunt Enid and Uncle Roy had been married for fifty-nine years. I affectionately referred to them as aunt and uncle as well. Aunt Enid wrote this letter to be shared with my dearest friend and her new husband on their wedding day.

Sheryl & Boniface

Thanks be to God for sparing our lives and making it worth living for these number of years, Giving us the opportunity to share with you our ideas of what True Love is.

True Love never dies. It grows, it blossoms as it matures with years. Love infuses the important element in all aspects of life. Love puts the beauty in everyday happenings—the warmth in a home, the joy in a memory, the "we" in a dream.

To accomplish successful longevity in marriage, it is essential to believe that no two people are alike. Therefore get to know each other well—your likes and dislikes—what makes each other happy or sad. Be patient, be considerate, be supportive, and always be ready to forgive.

Marriage vows are the most solemn in life and should be taken seriously. Bearing these in mind has kept us closely together for fifty-nine years—overcoming little problems, disagreements that may have flared up now and again.

God has not only guarded and guided us but protected us over the years, and we feel sure he'll do the same for you both.

May your marriage be blessed and may the Lord make you increase and abound in love for one another.

Sadly and unexpectedly, six months after my best friend was married, Aunt Enid and Uncle Roy died.

"They died on the same day, one hour apart, and were buried together, lying together in the same coffin. Even in death, they would not be apart," my best friend recalled.

"True Love never dies. It grows, it blossoms, as it matures with years."

— *Aunt Enid*

Roy and Enid Creary, married fifty-nine years
— Cherished Words

FINAL THOUGHTS ON
A LONG RELATIONSHIP

All the stories in this book I collected during my twenty-five-plus years of practice as an Emergency Medicine Physician in four different countries: the United States of America, Jamaica, New Zealand, and Australia. The storytellers told each one and are retold here to the best of my recollection. Many of the storytellers I was blessed to treat as patients. The stories are injected with candor, truth, humor, seriousness, and wit through tears and dry eyes, often in times of vulnerability. I am honored and appreciative of each person who allowed me a glimpse into their personal thoughts and lives.

I noted that no single theme emerged regarding relationship longevity in writing this book. But there appears to be a collaborative spirit, a willingness to participate, and plenty of give and take. The strength of the relationships didn't always lean toward the most vocal or the most ambitious. For some, the power of their relationship was their partner's small soft voice or the boldness of the other to take a leap of faith. Yes, faith seems to manifest itself around many corners—its belief and practice. But many traits seem to play a part in the longevity of many. From kindness to cherished words, eating together to separate vacations, friendship to romantic wit, longevity exists.

As you read these stories I hope that you will ponder them and reflect on your favorite ones. May they inspire you to contemplate the keys to longevity in your personal relationships.

ACKNOWLEDGMENTS

I am grateful for all the time that others have gifted me by reading and giving me feedback and ideas about this collection of stories.

I would be remiss if I did not provide a deep-felt thank you to two personal friends, Marisa Ressurreccion and Zenaida Rosario were extraordinary with their time. I am so honored that you both painstakingly read and reread my stories, and gave me support along with honest and insightful feedback. It was invaluable to me. A special "thank you" to my wonderful Sista'-friend, Dr. Sheryl Heron. I am grateful for your willingness to share the personal words of "our" Aunt and Uncle and am elated by your kind words and support in writing my Foreword. Your friendship over the years has been unwavering. To Kathy Negrelli, you have been burning the midnight oil from the beginning of my writings. You are such a constant in my life. A heartfelt thank you for your time and talent. As this endeavor unfolded, Karen Jacqueline, my partner, has been cheering me on and supportive beyond measure. I am truly grateful.

Sandy Draper, my editor, sounding board, and magic maker. You truly brought life to my book. So gracious and patient. I am delighted with your thoughtful suggestions, gentle nudges, keen insight, and time. Many, many thanks.

Thank you to friends and acquaintances who have shared their wisdom, insight and have indulged me as my vision for this book unfold.

Asya Blue - designer with vision. Thank you for sharing your talent and expertise.

I am blessed by the opportunity that God has given me as a physician, placed in a position to help and inspire others as we cross paths. I am incredibly appreciative and humbled by my patients and their willingness to be honest and open in sharing a small but significant glimpse of their life's journey with me. Their stories have encouraged me in my relationships, and I hope their stories touch the lives of many others.

ABOUT THE AUTHOR

D r. Patricia Baines grew up in Los Angeles, CA. She is an Emergency Medicine Physician who has spent over two decades as a physician and educator in the USA. She currently practices in Australia, and in her spare time, enjoys cooking, traveling, and reading. Her previous book, *Seven Days, The Journey Home,* is also a book centered on relationships, but of a different kind: particularly, one between herself and her nephew during unforeseen life-changing circumstances.